Rarely have we been pr[...]er
issues related to the jud[...]at
led to the crucifixion [...]a
fascinating story of the moral failings of Annas, Caiaphas, Pilate,
and Herod. The book is worthwhile for the historical information
alone, but the power of the book is found in the personal reflection
that is certain to happen. Character issues matter in the lives of leaders.
The virtues of justice, openness, fairness and courage are desperately
needed in our day. The implications for virtuous living and leadership
articulated by Gilmore are timely indeed. This is an important book
that should be widely read.

David S. Dockery
President
Union University,
Jackson, Tennessee

Modern historians are often strong on what happened in the past but
weak on its moral meaning. Gilmore seeks to discern both the facts
and the value of key legal proceedings that unfolded in the closing
hours of Christ's earthly life. Gilmore's work is imaginative,
informed, wise, and searching. He canvasses (mainly) the English
Bible and scholarly secondary sources to reconstruct a plausible
understanding of Jesus' trials. Gilmore clarifies many conundrums
and shows again that the New Testament accounts are empirically
compelling—and spiritually suggestive for readers with ears to hear.
I know of no better biographical approach to the trials of Jesus.

Bob Yarbrough
Trinity Evangelical Divinity School

Gilmore keeps us from being smug in our condescension at Caiaphas'
pathetic grasp at power, the Sanhedrin's gross bias, Pilate's trading
in the currency of injustice for the sake of political expediency, or
Herod's playboy distractions, by reminding us that we continue to
wallow in those same malfeasances today. He pointedly reminds that
no less than Justice William O. Douglas and the esteemed journalist
Bob Woodward have unveiled the occasional but troubling
misworkings of the United States Supreme Court. But Gilmore goes

beyond tracing the similarities between the judicial systems, something of enduring interest only to a lawyer or historian. It must be said, however, that for a lawyer, Gilmore's appendix containing a brief of due process violations at Christ's trials is worth the price of the book.

Gilmore never loses sight of the fact that, like the rest of scripture, the forensics matter only in what they teach us about orthodoxy and praxis, about God's person and our response. Gilmore's most important point is that, absent God's intervention, the same blindness that gripped Annas, Caiaphas, Herod Antipas, and Pilate and distorted those trials 2000 years ago, masks our eyes today. To deny that truth is to miss the whole point of (il)legalities.

Dr. Gilmore is not content simply to detail the legal maneuverings. He seeks to pierce through the layers of litigious wrappings to find the core motivations of those who 'tried' Christ. There he finds those influences that continue to drive our present interactions with the risen Lord. But just as Christ co-opted the jurisdiction of earthly courts, He continues to avoid our most urgent attempts to manacle him today.

It warms this lawyer's heart that with Gilmore's careful exposition, Christ's trials, bad ones at that, prove a rich source of exhortation.

Meirwyn I. Walters, Esq
Assistant Professor of Law,
Gordon College, Wenham, Massachusetts.

The Trials
of Christ

MORAL FAILINGS IN FOUR JUDGES

John Gilmore

Christian Focus

Dedicated to my three grand daughters:
Lauren Webster
Jenna Webster
Rachel Webster

Christian Focus Publications publishes biblically-accurate books for adults and children. The books in the adult range are published in three imprints.

Christian Heritage contains classic writings from the past.

Christian Focus contains popular works including biographies, commentaries, doctrine, and Christian living.

Mentor focuses on books written at a level suitable for Bible College and seminary students, pastors, and others; the imprint includes commentaries, doctrinal studies, examination of current issues, and church history.

For a free catalogue of all our titles, please write to

Christian Focus Publications,
Geanies House, Fearn,
Ross-shire, IV20 1TW, Great Britain

For details of our titles visit us on our web site
http://www.christianfocus.com

© John Gilmore
ISBN 1 85792 647 1

Published in 2001 by
Christian Focus Publications,
Geanies House, Fearn, Ross-shire
IV20 1TW, Great Britain

Cover design by Owen Daily

Printed and bound in Great Britain by
The Guernsey Press Co. Ltd., Guernsey, Channel Islands

Contents

Acknowledgments

I wish to thank Dr. Edwin Yamauchi of the Miami University (Oxford, Ohio, USA)'s History department for reading and commenting on an early draft of my work on the Trials of Christ. Also, special thanks to fellow Cincinnatian and neighbour, Newton Bush, Th.D., who read the work in its final stage, checking technical and transitional matters. On Scotland's side I wish to express my appreciation to Malcolm Maclean, my editor at Christian Focus Publications, who initially welcomed my pastoral contribution to biblical scholarship and has worked to see it in print. The Bible translation used at chapter heads is the New International Version, Copyright, 1984, International Bible Society.

PREFACE

My late father was not a lawyer, but like many non-lawyers, myself included, he was fascinated by matters of law. I have been present in a few courtrooms where civil cases have been conducted, and, now, to my delight my middle child, John Owen Gilmore, with one earned doctorate in science (Stanford University) is enrolled in Stanford's Law School in conjunction with his job as Technical Advisor of Intellectual Property at the law firm of Wilson Sonsini Goodrich & Rosati, Palo Alto, California. I find that lawyers, rather than deserving negative images and nasty humor, are greatly to be admired for a variety of reasons: first off, for their ability to 'go to the chase', to be concise in their comments, and always to be precise and avoid wordiness.

No other element of law draws me more than what Christ had to face before His four judges. To me and to countless other Christians that was the supreme case which, unlike many cases in modern times, did not drag on and on, with appeal after appeal. Yet in that brief span one finds mirror after mirror showing the complexity of the human psyche, especially of the elite. What Christ endured at two types of court – Jewish and Roman – we are privileged to read about from eye-witnesses through the faithful replication of those who had access to the original participants and their memories and accounts.

What follows is an attempt to grasp the gravity of what Christ faced, and its theological and practical applications. Other works are more technical. Yet what follows is based on many years of research and reflection. It is hoped that both the character of the judges, the tension of the interrogation scenes, and the divine composure of Jesus our Lord through it all come through for your enrichment and for your appreciation of the carefully written records of the four Gospels.

May God use these studies to sharpen your understanding of Christ's courtroom deportment, deepen your appreciation for His composure and strong witness under duress, and provide another dimension in which our New Testament records should be appreciated and admired.

Dr. John Gilmore
P. O. Box 24064
Cincinnati, OH 45224 USA

CHAPTER 1

INTRODUCTION

Jesus knew what it felt like to stand before a judge. He stood before several. The Gospel records give us an account of what happened to Jesus before four judges. In addition to the famous dual-functioning governor-judge, Pontius Pilate, whose name is repeated every Sunday where the Apostles' Creed is recited, there were the presiding judges of the Sanhedrin (the Jewish Supreme Court), Annas and his son-in-law successor, Joseph Caiaphas. (Incidentally, his first name is supplied by the first century Jewish historian, Josephus [AD 37-100]). Also, the secular ruler, Herod Antipas, judged Jesus.

Noteworthy in the Christian Gospels is the absence of bitterness and berating tone directed at the Jewish and Roman legal systems, despite their misuse in Jesus' execution. That Jesus' judges were controlled by evil did not result in New Testament writers demeaning legal, paralegal, and political positions. In contrast was eighteenth century evangelist George Whitefield who, in a letter dated May 7, 1739, expressed a view, now untypical among political evangelicals. He wrote: 'I think [being an attorney is] unlawful for a Christian.'[1]

Beside exhortations such as 'honor the king' (1 Peter 2:17c), Luke's expressions 'most excellent' (Luke 1:3; Acts 24:3; 26:25) showed respect for official rulers who were judicially powerful, if not juridically active. Luke dedicated his Gospel to one state official, a Christian named 'Theophilus' (see page 81).

Legal Backdrops in the New Testament
The average Christian should notice the importance of legal references in Scripture. Throughout the Old and New Testaments appear significant features of law, courts, and legal practice. The New Testament writers were not hesitant to imitate methods of argumentation, borrow forensic

imagery, adopt legal language, and hold to God's role as judge.[2]

Francis Lyall, Professor of Law at the University of Aberdeen, Scotland, has pursued legal metaphors in the New Testament epistles.[3] His studies range across references to slaves and freedmen, aliens and citizens, adoption and the inheritance that went with it, redemption and the new legal relationships with God for the Christian.

That a legal mind-set was not anti-Christian appears in an allusion Jesus used in the Gospel of John. The Greek word *parakletos* suggested elementary emotional support through legal guidance. Greek law courts required a defendant to plead his case in person, though they allowed professional writers to assist in preparing his defence. Moreover, the defendant was allowed to have someone, called a *parakletos*, to stand by his side, to give him moral support, to prompt him in technical points, and to instruct him how best to meet his opponent's case. Latin authors translated the Greek word *parakletos* as *advocatus*, but, admittedly, the use of *parakletos* as lawyer in the fullest sense was rare.[4] Our Lord told His disciples that the Holy Spirit would be a *parakletos*-person (John 14:16). Jesus intimated that the Spirit would prosecute His claims, authority, and words (John 15:26; 16:8-11).

Legal Aspects in John

The Gospel of John is structured after legal interests and studded with sustained legal interaction.[5] The Gospel opens with a judicial deputation seeking a deposition (1:19-28) that both anticipated and illustrated Jesus' later examination by the same Sanhedrin (18:12-14, 19-24).

The vigorous cross-examination in John 5:31-40, on a local level, similarly reflected the strong desire to establish the guilt of Jesus. John 8 records a conversational interchange between Jesus and His critics. The dialogue shows an accelerating intensity to isolate Jesus as an offender. A chapter-length story (John 9) on the healing of a man born blind reflects a Pharisee-conducted, full-scale investigation of Jesus and not just of His supporters. About this C. H. Dodd wrote:

> As sheer drama, this trial scene is one of the most brilliant passages in the Gospel, rich in tragic irony of which the evangelist is master.[6]

Against the background of Jesus being relentlessly hassled by Jewish authorities is the theme of witness. Of particular importance in John is the word 'witness'. There it is a sub-theme.[7] Many episodes in John are reported in the formal character of a case at law.[8]

Further Legal Allusions

Although the Gospel records of Christ's trials are not replete with legal terminology, on points of law the narrators were familiar with distinctions, such as the steps in the reprimand of local synagogue law in John 9[9] and in the gradation of beatings in Christ's trials before Pilate.[10] Yet there are aspects of the trial narratives which lack technical precision, such as the question of whether Pilate pronounced a verdict or not[11] and whether 'to send' (Luke 23:7, 11, 15; Philemon 12), especially in Jesus' trial section, had the technical connotation of officially sending to Caesar (Acts 25:21).[12] A certain degree of imprecision always accompanies a popular style.

Blinzler, author of one of the two best works on Christ's trials, has noted:

> The gospels ... are concerned, not to produce a detailed report, but to show the significance of the events for the salvation of mankind.[13]

Missing Items in the Gospels

The Gospel versions of the trials have noticeable gaps. There are pieces of information missing. John, for instance, omitted the Caiaphas-conducted trial and conflated Jesus' two appearances before Pilate into one. The conversations between Jesus and Pilate, though fuller than in the Synoptic Gospels, were, nevertheless, only pertinent excerpts. Some transitional clues and chronological correlations were kept to a minimum. Even at that, however, the Gospels contain a proportionately large amount of material on Christ's last week.

Omissions in the Present Study

In order to fit the aims of this introductory study of Christ's judges, several important Passion sub-plots have been omitted: such as Jesus' arrest, the denials of Peter, the Barabbas Easter-clemency story, Pilate's wife's dream and her influence, the role of Judas, the beatings, scourging and mockery of Christ, the sentencing, and the crucifixion itself. What has been covered amounts to the pivotal segments. These Passion vignettes regarding His final week and days, of course, are integral to the whole. They have been ignored, not because they are not important, but because the intent has been to let the larger pictures stand center stage.

Why so Much Space to Jesus' Trials?

Why have the Four Gospels devoted so much space to Jesus' trials? Proportionately, our Lord's last week gets more lines than does the rest of His life. To the early church, the way in which everything converged at the end was an essential part of the 'good news' or gospel.

The Evangelists were faithful to historical phases and facts. Through them they intended to involve the reader in dealing with the dimension of evil's sinisterness and subtlety. In the Gospels we are exposed to the dynamics involved in the silencing of righteousness by those threatened by it.

So long as the documents are valued as primary documents in Christ's trials they will also be windows in our understanding of human behavior. Their role is similar to a prism that sorts out and shows, at the same time, the separate glories of Christ and the separate negative emotions and moral bent directing, shaping, and fuelling the silencing of Christ.

What transpired in the Evangelists' accounts endures. Besides showing the glory of Christ in crisis, the Gospels bare the human heart. Jesus' claim and character brought out what was in man. The narratives expose human under-handedness, deviousness and self-protective double-standards. Admittedly, the Gospels present the chief characters of Christ's passion in dark colours, for to calculate, implement, and conclude such an outrageous plot had the trademark of Satanic involvement.

Where do modern readers stand in relationship to this Christ so foully abused, so horribly assaulted, and so unjustly executed? Surely, Jesus' accusers acted prejudicially in remembering details; His judges acted perfunctorily in complying with legal procedure; and His captors acted perversely in executing justice. But what do the intricate manoeuvring, secret sessions, suppression of evidence, distortion of facts, in-court and out-of-court beatings, switching of charges, and omission of fairness say not only *to* us but *of* us? Are there not invisible but real ties between Sadducean aristocrats, who thirsted for Jesus' death, and American middle-class attitudes, which are pleased with His non-interference in lives?

Historical studies, of necessity, require care, especially careful avoidance of moralizing. Indeed, the Four Gospels tell their story of the trials that way. Jesus' scourging (found in the Four Gospels), for instance, was told briefly and with great reserve. This part of Christ's sufferings could have been written judgmentally. The Evangelists, however, recorded the facts sympathetically, yet factually.

What follows tries to maintain the accuracy, concreteness, and objectivity of the Gospels. The bias and bigotry of the judges stand out. Local animosity has seeped through into the charges filed.

Readers would do well, however, to go a step beyond the dimension of historical detail and emerge into the area of personal analysis and autobiographical application.

This, of course, was also the intention of the Gospel writers. And their story was told with such crispness and selective completeness so as to involve us in pulling back the curtain on human motivations, hypocrisy, and demonic hatred.

The dynamic of man being confronted by God in the person of His Son is humbling and heart-searching. The continuing relevance of the events and their ability to facilitate a dissection of the human psyche cannot be underestimated.

Unless we advance to self-scrutiny we have missed a major benefit. We must go from reading to reflection, from historical investigation to spiritual evaluation, or by default we participate in our own impoverishment. A study of Christ's trials can turn into an escape mechanism by which we try to avoid our own judgment. We must recognize that the responses of the original participants were typically human responses, embarrassingly similar-to-us personal responses.

The rewards of meditating upon the trials of Christ far exceed a rigorous chronicle of them. Through the chambers of justice, Jewish and Roman, we enter into an arena of understanding which far surpasses a holy place and holy times mind-set. We are exposed to a new dimension of self-analysis led by narrators of Christ's last week.

Getting facts straight
Two Jewish and two Roman judges interrogated Jesus: Annas, the retired High Priest; Joseph Caiaphas, his successor; Pontius Pilate; and Herod Antipas. But how many times did He appear before them?

One Trial, Four or More?
A minor issue, of course, is whether Christ endured one trial or four trials. Many choose to describe it as a single trial, others, like myself, prefer to refer to 'Christ's trial*s*'.

One reason for the hesitation to speak of trial*s* is because His appearance before Annas lacked legal status. There is justifiable reason to say, however, that Christ's appearance before Annas (subject of chapter 2), should still be classed as one of the trials. True, it wasn't technically part of the proceedings, yet John thought it significant to include it. Without it the sinister aspect of Jesus' removal would be less definite and the emotional need to have Jesus erased would be less understood. The impression is strong that Annas was no less Satanically motivated than Judas.

In his seminal work on this subject, Josef Blinzler pointed out that the language of John carefully preserved the private character of Jesus' appearance before the emeritus high priest (John 18:13). The meeting was unofficial.[14]

How Many Sessions?
A full counting of Jesus' time in court would add to, not reduce the number of sessions, for in point of fact, Jesus appeared before his earthly judges, not five, but at least *six* times – three meetings with Jewish judges and three meetings with Roman judges!

What went on in that additional third Jewish meeting?

Since Annas' meeting with Jesus was more personal than professional, and since the examination of Jesus by Caiaphas was at night without the necessary court quorum, a special session was hastily arranged. Jesus was brought before the Great Sanhedrin, when a quorum could be *assembled* in early dawn (Mark 15:1; Matt. 27:1; Luke 22:66ff.). This was the 'only legal and plenary one'[15] where a quorum of twenty-three (a minimum number) out of a total court of seventy-one could be convened. [16]

Sanhedrin in Seating and Procedures[17]

Judaism's Supreme Court, the Great Sanhedrin, had forty-six elders, composed of lay nobility, members of both Pharisees, the popular party, and Sadducees. The Sanhedrin was seventy-one members strong, including the high priest.

The early morning meeting of the Sanhedrin will not be examined separately in this study. According to the *Mishnah* (section: 'Sanhedrin,' iv.3) they regularly sat on a raised platform in the shape of a semicircle, allowing each member to see the other.

The elders sat in the outer circle, a rim of several rows. The centre was occupied by twenty-four priests, the clerical aristocracy. Most priests in the Sanhedrin were Sadducees. Outside the Sanhedrin some priests were Pharisees. Like the Sanhedrin Sadducees, the Sanhedrin Pharisees were rich and represented eminent families. Wealthy Pharisee Joseph of Arimathea, a Jesus sympathizer, supplied the unused stone tomb for Jesus' burial and resurrection.

The President sat on the western end of the chamber facing the court, flanked by former high priests Annas, Ismael, Eleasar, and Simon. Thus when a justice spoke, the others could see and hear him.

And the early morning, final, full-quorum Sanhedrin

validation of Jesus' condemnation, the Sanhedrin violated its own practice and rule of not pronouncing condemnation until the next day. Each justice present, from the youngest to the oldest, was to stand, give his vote, and have his vote recorded in writing. Before Jesus was taken to Pilate, this procedure was, undoubtedly, followed.

At this brief session two points of business were handled:

1. The ratification of the previous verdict in the hastily-called, partial quorum Sanhedrin session.[18]

2. The recasting of the indictment from blasphemy, which was not usually punished by death in the Roman court, to that of a political offence against the State, which was.[19]

Other Venue Questions

More questions revolve around Christ's trials than just their number. Some would wish detailed attention were given to scheduling, time factors, and chronology. References are made here to these in a limited way. Still others would like more space allowed for dealing with place and jurisdiction matters.

Where these events took place does have importance. But in this treatment they are hardly touched upon, except as they have some moral application. Thus, questions of time and place aren't examined in any depth. The reader is encouraged to consult those books recommended in the *Selected Bibliography*, immediately following the *End Notes*.

The Critical Issue of Historical Accuracy

Deeper and far more crucial is the matter of the integrity of the New Testament record in reportage. A few comments on this important matter are required.

A Jewish scholar, Ellis Rivkin, in *What Crucified Jesus? (The Political Execution of a Charismatic),* holds to a low view of the historic reliability of the Four Gospels with special doubts about the value of John.[20] He wrote:

> These portraits [i.e., the Four Gospels] are so at variance that we cannot be certain which is the most lifelike.[21]

Space and time won't allow a detailed addressing of this issue, yet we cannot ignore or consider it inconsequential. Careful examinations of the Gospels by numerous scholars are available. Of particular value are those works which deal with the details of the biblical text, rather than the writings of authors who make sweeping statements without substantiation.

The series of events regarding Jesus' trials in the gospel accounts are not jumbled and mistakenly juxtaposed. Rather, despite some gaps, they present a coherent and cogent reflection of what took place.

Christianity makes much of the credibility of its theology, because it is rooted in history. Some, however, dismiss the historical references in the Gospels as part of the scheme of rationalizing Jesus' messianic and deity claims.

> Modern criticism has pointed out that the passion narratives of our gospels are less dominated by apologetic motives. One must not, however, exaggerate the apologetic streak in them, as is often done.[22]

How Reliable is the Gospel of John?

The Gospel of John in particular has been unfairly judged as *twistory*, not history. Rivkin, mentioned earlier, said John 'elevates Jesus out of his historical setting onto a timeless plane'.[23] Since in our presentation of Christ's trials/judges John gets special emphasis, some comments on John's trustworthiness are in order.

> John's predilection for stressing the traits of Jesus which show His majesty is no argument that these were invented by him; all the less so since Mark's description of the demeanour of Jesus is essentially the same (cf. the arrest, Mark 14:42, 48ff.; the trial, 14:62).[24]

A.N. Sherwin-White, an expert in ancient Roman law, considered John's trial references to be historically reliable:

> After the survey of the legal and administrative background, it is apparent that there is no historical improbability in the Johannine variations of this sort from the synoptic version.[25]

Further examination of this important issue requires outside reading. I have suggested some works to be read on this matter in order to aid those readers wishing to pursue this further. See end note 26.

The Corollary Controversy: Alleged Anti-Jewishness

The matter of alleged anti-semitism in the New Testament documents is considered more important than whether or not the Gospels had historical flaws. Of course, the two issues are inter-related.

I hold that the Gospels were not anti-semitic. An anti-Jewishness cannot be established from the New Testament. My reasons for taking this position are found in the Appendix.

Dr. Blinzler's comment provides the right balance:

[The Gospels] betray the effort to underline heavily the guilt of the Jews in the death of Jesus, with the result that the guilt of the Romans does not always emerge with sufficient sharpness. This tendency has to be kept in view by anyone who undertakes to reconstruct the course of events. The evangelists achieve this shifting of the accent, however, only by leaving out here and there things which could more or less exonerate the Jews. On the other hand, it cannot be proved that they inserted anti-Jewish stories invented for the purpose. The inclination, frequently to be observed, to condemn as unhistorical or at least suspicious everything in the light of the passion story which throws an unfavourable light on the Jews, has to be met with the question: 'Whence, then, came the boundless anti-Semitism attributed to primitive Christianity if the Jews had little or nothing to do with the death of Jesus?' The first believers and the original transmitters of the gospel narratives were all of Jewish origin themselves. The story of the passion, which was largely missionary in its purpose and aimed in fact particularly at the conversion of the Jews, would have failed in its missionary effect had it contained anti-Jewish particulars which would inevitably have been shown up sooner or later as an invention.[27]

Evidence from Outside the New Testament

An ancient letter, written near the start of the Christian era by an avowed non-Christian Syrian, named Mara bar Sarapion, supports the view that the Gospel's presentations of Christ's passion were not spin-offs of deliberate bias. Josef Blinzler, who cites the text of the letter, concluded:

Since ... no trace of Christian influence can be detected in him, his allusion represents a valuable proof that, at that time, even non-Christian circles in Syria credited the Jews with the decisive part in the execution of Jesus.[28]

Key persons masterminded Jesus' arrest, trial, and death. Mark, often regarded as the first Gospel to be written, takes unjust blame for setting an anti-Jewish tone, or trying to make Rome look good to Roman readers, and of making the fledgling Christian Church look good by going easy on the Romans.[29] Mention of Sanhedrinist involvement was not meant to single out the Jewish race for what happened. The final question is not the degree of guilt borne by Jews and Romans together or separately, but the power of Christ's death to remove human guilt in the generations then, and since then.

> The Cross sheds no light at all on biology or race. It does, however, shed a flood of light on the sin of the human heart, and sin is a malady which involves all mankind.[30]

Christ's trials are incomprehensible unless seen in their original context. Nothing can compensate when the biblical record is neglected. What is found in the Four Gospels gives the fuller picture. The present study focuses on their essential features with application to human behaviour today.

The judge before whom Jesus first appeared was the one who most sought to destroy him. Heading the trials was the preliminary hearing before Annas, the ex-high priest, the subject of the next chapter.

CHAPTER 2

CHRIST BEFORE ANNAS

John 18:12-14, 19-24

¹²Then the detachment of soldiers with its commander and the Jewish officials arrested Jesus. They bound him ¹³and brought him first to Annas, who was the father-in-law of Caiaphas, the high priest that year. ¹⁴Caiaphas was the one who had advised the Jews that it would be good if one man died for the people.

¹⁹Meanwhile, the high priest questioned Jesus about his disciples and his teaching.

²⁰ 'I have spoken openly to the world,' Jesus replied. 'I always taught in synagogues or at the temple, where all the Jews come together. I said nothing in secret. ²¹Why question me? Ask those who heard me. Surely they know what I said.'

²²When Jesus said this, one of the officials nearby struck him in the face. 'Is this the way you answer the high priest?' he demanded.

²³ 'If I said something wrong,' Jesus replied, 'testify as to what is wrong. But if I spoke the truth, why did you strike me?'

²⁴ Then Annas sent him, still bound, to Caiaphas the high priest.

Frequently, Jesus' trials are conflated or lumped together. This is especially true of the records of Christ's interrogation before Annas and before Joseph Caiaphas. Since John's is the only Gospel containing Annas' interrogation of Jesus, many assume John's reference to Annas was historically inaccurate, that the writer had confused Jesus' appearance before Annas with His appearance before Caiaphas.

Such a conclusion, however, makes the use of John for other information questionable. Was Annas' stature less than Caiaphas'? Or was it not rather the reverse – that Caiaphas was putty in the hands of retired Annas? Although no longer its president and presiding judge, Annas' imprint and impact upon the Sanhedrin was enormous.

Annas had been the high priest of Judaism's supreme court from AD 6 to 15. Because Rome had conquered Israel, the Jews lost their former right to appoint their chief official, the high priest. (It would be equivalent to having our President selected by foreign invaders). Annas was put in office by Quirinius, the governor of Syria, 'about the time Judea was reduced to the status of a minor Roman province.'[1]

Annas was forced out of office nine years later by Valerius Gratus, Pilate's predecessor. But his influence, however, continued undiminished.

The office conferred a certain permanency by which a high priest retained not only the title, but many special privileges and obligations of the office *after the end of his tenure.*[2]

Annas' clout among Jews and Romans alike was colossal. In ten years Annas made many friends and developed a network of power politics. In addition to having Joseph Caiaphas, his son-in-law, as his replacement, he had five sons who later attained the rank of high priest!

Klaas Schilder, who has produced the only theological interpretation of the trial, summed up Annas' stature: 'He

27

was the father of a generation of priests and even the founder of a dynasty of high priests.'[3]

Moreover, he used his enormous wealth to buy favours and further his own ends. Rome had charge of appointing the high priest and it went to the highest bidder.

> The prolonged ascendancy of the house of Annas is an evidence no less of their corruption than of their astuteness.[4]

One cash gift to a covetous Roman governor would mean that further favours required additional money. It was likely that special favours were done on the quiet for wealthy Annas and Caiaphas because they greased the palms of Pilate. Although there is no record of such transactions with Pilate, there were two opportunities where a cash-advance would have been likely:

1. In arranging a contingency of Roman soldiers at Jesus' arrest (John 18:12, *speira* or cohort, 200 men, and *chiliarch*, officer in charge of 1000, equivalent to an Army Colonel)

2. In the placing of Roman guards at Jesus' tomb (Matt. 27:64, 65; 28:11-15).

Payments under the table involved additional meetings. Frank Morison argued that on the eve of Jesus' arrest, 'some kind of communication with Pilate was inevitable'.[5] If his suggestion is right, then when Caiaphas went to see Pilate, Caiaphas had in mind to secure the promise of troops, extra forces to ensure Jesus' capture, and forthrightly let Pilate know their intentions against Jesus.

Support for this idea is deduced from historical patterns, but also from biblical allusion. For instance, there is strong likelihood that Pilate clearly understood that Jesus was delivered because of Sanhedrin jealousy (Mark 15:10), which he learned from a private meeting. John 18:34, moreover, seems to indicate that Jesus knew of these secret negotiations between Pilate and the Annas/Caiaphas connection, and He let Pilate know He knew.

If, as we suppose, an unrecorded visit took place, bribe money may have been used to secure Pilate's co-operation, since goodwill alone would not have done it. (After all, Pilate had a deep contempt for Jews, John 18:35; 19:14, 15).

If such transactions ensured additional forces in Jesus' arrest, and the stakes were high in what was in progress, then Annas was too close to personal victory over Jesus to refuse to go one step further and have his son-in-law pay a visit on Pilate when he was conducting a preliminary hearing.

> There seems to be no doubt that it was the practice in some cases for the High Priest to communicate personally with the Procurator and make representations about an impending trial.[6]

Officially, Annas was retired, but emotionally, he was 'in'. Though no longer on the bench, he quietly exerted pressure. He was the Sanhedrin's trusted advisor who had become a legend in the Jewish priestly aristocracy.

Need someone out of office be past his prime? Caiaphas, the actual reigning high priest, certainly looked upon Annas as an asset, although others may have thought him too old to help.

> Annas was a man having a seasoned experience; he had been called upon to act in difficult cases before, and had developed a technique in the art of finding official formulas and procedures. This man, surely, would be invaluable to Caiaphas in defining the arguments, formulating the charge, striking out irrelevant matters, and, in short, quickly directing litigation to the main issues. The old man's advice would make the work of Caiaphas just so much easier.[7]

Christ was first brought to Annas. Here is a clue concerning Annas' desire and drive for an active involvement in the affair of Jesus. He had no right to have the accused brought to him, but Annas had his way. This facet suggests that Annas' position was strong in the eyes of Caiaphas, if not in the eyes of Rome.

The meeting was unofficial. It was an interview, rather than a real trial. As A. E. Harvey has noted, it was 'an entirely informal investigation'.[8] Some see its function as that of a grand jury. If Jesus' next trial (before the Sanhedrin conducted by Caiaphas) was equivalent to a grand jury proceeding, determining the charge, then Jesus' appearance before Annas was of the order of a hearing in the quarters of the police. Ernst Bammel was careful to note, however, that it was not a formal hearing, but an attempt by Annas to extract from Jesus details which 'might result in the persecution of the disciples'.[9]

Jesus was examined in the presence of a guard-servant and 'possibly of some other hierarchs'.[10]

What importance could the interrogation have had? It would have seemed more important to Annas for at least two reasons:

First, it would give him the satisfaction of confronting the Teacher whose activities gave him so much distress.

Annas undoubtedly took delight in seeing Jesus bound before him. He had followed the various exhibitions of hatred which had been directed against Jesus with a sympathetic interest; in fact, he had taken an active part in these. Hence it was a source of grim pleasure to the old aristocrat finally to see the man before him who – in his estimation – had almost started a revolution against the authority of the priesthood.[11]

It must have made Annas gloat, because he was finally on the verge of settling a personal score.

But secondly, and more significantly, it would enable him

to enlarge the purge to include Jesus' disciples, who by administrative oversight got away.

Jesus was probably taken to the palace of Caiaphas, which is still in existence. It was likely that Caiaphas allowed Annas a room for interrogation that night, even if Annas didn't actually reside there. Some have suggested that Annas probably lived in a wing of the palace, which was connected by a common courtyard.[12] Some, however, would not be sure about the location, and would not extend the probability beyond a luxurious mansion located in the Upper City.[13]

Jesus was brought bound, tightly tied. We would say that He was handcuffed. The language of John 18:12 and 18:24 suggests that though Jesus was brought bound to the hearing, His restraints were undone indoors, and then replaced, following the session, before being transferred to Caiaphas.[14]

But all through the hearing one has the impression that more serious bindings went unseen.

The Law was Bound
The Great Sanhedrin operated as the highest court of Jewish law.[15] It was composed of seventy-one members: seventy judges and one presiding jurist, the president of the court, the high priest. Of the seventy members twenty-four were members of the clerical aristocracy, all priests. These sat closest to the chair of the presiding justice. The other members were from the lay nobility, forty-six elders. The next chapter treats Christ's appearance before this court. It is enough to note that the Great Sanhedrin could and did engage in illegalities. (See the Appendix for detailed information on legal matters).

Recall in John 11:49-50, Caiaphas, the presiding judge said: 'It is expedient for you that one man should die for the people and that the whole nation should not perish' (NASB).

That meant that Jesus' conviction and death was a foregone conclusion, which all through *John* Jesus anticipated (5:18; 7:1, 25, 30, 44; 8:20, 59; 10:31, 39; 11:51). John reminds his readers of this in the retelling of Jesus' appearance before Annas (18:14).

Several other points of law were violated at this stage:

1. Annas, as an ex-high priest, was out of order to prosecute;
2. The arrest was unjustifiable, because He was not charged with a capital offence;
3. An arrest at night was illegal;
4. Roman soldiers were involved;
5. The blow upon Jesus' face during the examination was a travesty of justice, entirely unwarranted and unfair.

Annas was Bound

Annas was bound not simply by the natural frailty which comes to those past seventy, but he was bound, in addition, by family and financial ties. These kept his interest keen in the outcome of Jesus' arraignment.

But Annas was bound, not only in the sense that he felt a legal and familial obligation to see the case through, and to assist in its progress and success, but he was bound in a way which never crossed his mind.

1. Annas was bound by pride

Annas was a living symbol of prosperity. He had spotless loyalty to Sadducean traditions and to Sanhedrin control. In our culture, he would be a senior executive who receives commemorative plaques and company prizes. His record and reputation were unmatched. He was known for 'his uncommon energy and great gifts as a diplomatist'.[16]

Annas was a chancellor figure. He epitomized the spirit of the world-system which was in opposition to God. Jesus linked speaking in the world and the synagogues as the same act (John 18:20 – 'I spoke openly to the world; I always taught in the synagogue').

Annas perceived Jesus' addresses as 'secret', because only to those proud persons like him were Jesus' open and plain insights dark or 'secret' to them. Unbelief would interpret Jesus' statements as dark (John 8:43). Because Annas admired his own importance, prestige, and power, he represented the world of darkness as much as Pilate or Herod Antipas.

2. Annas was bound by greed

Annas' wealth was vast.[17] He, undoubtedly, had devised financial schemes which brought him enormous riches. He was a business man in addition to being the high priest. Two out of his three sons at this stage of his career were Temple treasurers.[18]

When the Roman general Titus destroyed Jerusalem in 70, Annas' personal fortune amounted to two and one-half billion pieces of silver. Annas' assets grew from the revenue from inflated prices for sacrificial animals sold at Passover.[19]

Conceivably, Annas could have used, in getting favours, those who were delinquent in repaying loans to him, even if he did not, outright, bribe accomplices in the Roman government.

Though priest, he hadn't taken any vow of poverty, for he had his fingers in the Temple treasury. In effect, his hand was on the bank vault door, if the keys were not on his ring.

3. Annas was bound by hate

Jesus cleansed the Temple twice (see Appendix 2). The first was at the start of His ministry; the last during His last week.

Both occasions greatly angered Annas, for in cleansing the Temple twice Jesus had interfered with Annas' and Caiaphas' enormous money-making project. Too little emphasis has been placed on how the cleansings fuelled the movement to get rid of Jesus. The cleansings acted like catapults in launching the ambition of the Sanhedrin to destroy Jesus.

Annas was determined to get even with Jesus for spoiling his income from the Temple. Reprisal was planned for the man who attacked their financial interests. Jesus had made inroads into the body of Judaism and, as they saw it, it had to be halted.

Hatred for Christ first began with the social upper crust.

All who belonged to the upper strata of society ... were inimical to Jesus.[20]

The contempt Annas had for Jesus was partially reflected in His suspicions about His disciples and about the so-called secret teachings Jesus peddled. But Jesus denied that He was attempting to establish a secret society. He said plainly:

I have spoken openly to the world. I always taught in synagogues or at the temple, where all the Jews come together. I said nothing in secret (John 18:20, NIV).

4. Annas was bound by deceit

Annas accused Jesus of secrecy when *he* was the one who was secretive. Annas exercised thought-control over the Sanhedrin for years, first by his presence and later by his reputation. Annas' opinions, conclusions, and quiet urgings rippled like thunder through the Court.

It appears that Caiaphas became the mouthpiece and sounded the pitch set by Annas. Though Caiaphas showed personal independence, nevertheless he shared with Annas a

Christ Before Annas

common dislike for Jesus. They were in cahoots for Jesus' arrest, sentencing, and execution. Annas' methods were underhanded, his motives cloaked, his plottings sinister, and his aims demonic.

Jesus, in contrast, had nothing to hide. New doctrines were allowed in the Temple courtyard. Jewish tradition encouraged the free expression of ideas. Annas, however, did not want Jesus' free access to the people to continue.

Christ was Bound

Jesus was treated as a common criminal. To tie Him was to show Him contempt. It was a cowardly measure, which maliciously insinuated that Jesus was dangerous. Jesus' reaction was peaceful and untainted by the spirit of retaliation. Yet at the same time it should be noted that Jesus would not let a clear violation of law slip by without a vigorous protest (John 18:23).

Christ did not cower before Annas. In this He was untypical of anyone who had previously appeared before the high priest. Josephus related how the accused in Jewish courts were expected to assume a servile, beaten look.[21] They were expected to plead for mercy, not protest against injustice. Jesus' response to abuse by the attending guard had no view to soften the judge. There, His reply 'must have seemed disrespectful and offensive'.[22]

Christ was not bound by the sin which kept the ex-high priest captive. Jesus was not held in tow or in need of taming by those restraints.

If we are to look for Christ's bonds, we are not to look at His hands. He was bound in heart and mind to accomplishing the will of His Father. He came to do God's will. He had volunteered. It was not a binding against His will.

By immobilizing Jesus physically, they could not strip Him

35

of His power, nor could they permanently smear His character. The binding was the beginning of dehumanizing Jesus. They were deceived into thinking that the cords of hemp, as later they were to think the bands of death, could hold Him.

To detain was to debase, to manacle was to mock, and to immobilize was to isolate. But Jesus was not bound by sin, but by sinners. Jesus was captive but not criminal. He had a free hand in His own destiny. Near the conclusion of the charade of justice, Christ told Pilate,

You would have no authority over Me, unless it had been given you from above (John 19:11, NASB).

All through the Gospel of John Jesus had shown Himself to be in charge. His Passion was the triumph of light over darkness. What selective Jewish hierarchs thought their victory was in fact Jesus' victory/ascension, for in John's Gospel, 'going up' to the cross and 'lifted up' upon the cross was part and parcel of our Lord's enthronement and exaltation. His glory was demonstrated in conflict and in the lying denunciation of His opponents. His crucifixion was being lifted up in exaltation and His cross became His throne.

Constraint, rather than restraint, characterized Jesus. He was constrained to follow His Father's plan. He was more in the bosom of the Father than in the grip of His foes.

Jesus' captors never comprehended His divine identity and capability of destroying them. Unjust detention and cruel restraints used against Him could have been broken. He who raised the dead could strike dead. He who drove away demons could command angels (Matt. 26:53). He who could walk on water could trample His assailants. He who could heal could also maim.

But it was love which held Jesus. It was love for His Father and His glory. Also, we cannot forget, it was love for us that kept Him on course. God was determined to bring to faith those given to Christ, from eternity (John 17:6, 9).

What kept His power in check was not leather thongs, but His love for His own, and for His Father. He endured many injustices in order that we might share in and be recipients of His righteousness.

It was pitiful and paradoxical for Christ to be bound. But it was just as paradoxical to see Annas free. He thought he had a free hand in shuttling Jesus to oblivion, yet in fact Annas was not free, but held by his inveterate sinfulness and by a demonic desire to revenge Jesus' attempt to right the capsized ship of Judaism.

In the character of Annas are reflected rays of the modern religious hypocrite whose reputation, on the surface, is without one damaging shadow, but whose entire mind-set seals off and shuts out the true reign, the true rule of Scripture over self.

Are we like Annas? Do we secretly bind Jesus so He won't meddle in our lives and remould our thinking? Are our thoughts in captivity to Christ?

> Wicked men strive in prayer more to get off their chains than to get off their sins; more to be delivered from enemies without than lusts within.[23]

Are we wanting to be freed *of* Christ or freed *by* Christ? Without Christ in our lives we are locked into a closed system where no one is over self. A self-dominated life brings temporary contentment, but not lasting peace.

Granted that we are all set upon by drives and desires which keep us in bondage, we must face the matter of how we can be freed. We must look outside ourselves to Christ, who, when the clock of God's decrees struck 'go-free', the strongest restraint, death, could not hold Him.

Coming from under the inhibiting power of sin is not within our jurisdiction. It is out of our field. It is not something we can do. Cutting us free from sin is a work done *in* us by God, not a work done *by* us. Charles Wesley's lines explain the need of divine intervention and the action of saving grace:

Long my imprisoned spirit lay
Fast bound in sin and nature's night.
Thine eye diffused a quickening ray,
I woke, the dungeon flamed with light;
My chains fell off, my heart was free,
I rose, went forth, and followed Thee.

CHAPTER 3

CHRIST BEFORE
JOSEPH CAIAPHAS

[57]Those who had arrested Jesus took him to Caiaphas, the high priest, where the teachers of the law and the elders had assembled. [58]But Peter followed him at a distance, right up to the courtyard of the high priest. He entered and sat down with the guards to see the outcome.

[59]The chief priests and the whole Sanhedrin were looking for false evidence against Jesus so that they could put him to death. [60]But they did not find any, though many false witnesses came forward.

Finally two came forward [61]and declared, 'This fellow said, "I am able to destroy the temple of God and rebuild it in three days."'

[62]Then the high priest stood up and said to Jesus, 'Are you not going to answer? What is this testimony that these men are bringing against you?' [63]But Jesus remained silent.

The high priest said to him, 'I charge you under oath by the living God: Tell us if you are the Christ, the Son of God.'

[64] 'Yes, it is as you say,' Jesus replied. 'But I say to all of you: In the future you will see the Son of Man sitting at the right hand of the Mighty One and coming on the clouds of heaven.'

[65]Then the high priest tore his clothes and said, 'He has spoken blasphemy! Why do we need any more witnesses? Look, now you have heard the blasphemy. [66]What do you think?'

'He is worthy of death,' they answered.

[67]Then they spat in his face and struck him with their fists. Others slapped him [68]and said, 'Prophesy to us, Christ. Who hit you?'

See also Mark 14:53-65; Luke 22:63-71

Following Jesus' appearance before Annas, the ex-high priest, He was taken to another room in Caiaphas' palace the same night. The meeting was hastily called. Many members could not make it. There was not enough for a quorum.

Joseph Caiaphas presided over this session. Lacking a quorum,[1] they felt duty bound to call for a full session early the next morning, at which time they could finalize the previous evening's decision and plan the next strategy. Despite the poor attendance the Sanhedrin session continued with Caiaphas in the chair as presiding judge.

Sanhedrin location

Ordinarily, the seventy-one member Supreme Court of Judaism met in the Hall of Hewn Stone, which was next to the Temple, to the north and east of the high priest's palace. It was *there*, in all likelihood, that the early morning meeting of the Sanhedrin met in full quorum (Mark 15:1; Matt. 27:1; Luke 22:66-23:1). But the previous hasty trial conducted by Caiaphas was probably in his official residence.

Numerous infractions of their own laws were made in getting rid of Jesus. Even before the trials began, important Sanhedrin regulations were ignored in order to achieve their aim. For instance, for Caiaphas to convene the court in his home was illegal. Other violations were committed: to hold court on the eve of a holy day was illegal; to hold court at night was illegal; to hold court without a quorum was illegal. These were just the beginning of illegalities. It showed how much Jesus was hated – the hatred compelling judges to avoid honouring the law, and driving priests to seek vengeance. (For a fuller listing of illegalities, see the Appendix 1).

Who was Caiaphas and what was he like? In the previous chapter we noted that Annas was Caiaphas' predecessor and father-in-law. They worked in close association. Caiaphas was the high priest and president of the Great Sanhedrin.

41

Caiaphas' Identity

The office of high priest was comparable to being President of the nation. The Jewish state culminated in Caiaphas. 'He was its highest authority, its living representative.'[2]

For a time Caiaphas was probably under the tutelage, even thumb, of the older Annas. Some hold that while Caiaphas was the actual high priest, he was only the nominal head of the Sanhedrin, and that Annas was the virtual head.[3] In their conqueror status, the Romans cancelled the Jewish tradition in which high priests were elected for life. The Romans abolished the practice and policy of lifelong high priests. This was a procedural measure to keep the position weak, when formerly it was strong. But Rome only broke up the tradition; it did not really loosen the grip of the high priest.[4]

The Sanhedrin's decisions were Annas-animated. Although John's Gospel bypassed the opportunity to comment on the degree of Annas' influence, it was already widely known. But that was not to say that Caiaphas was a puppet or rubber stamp.

Caiaphas had a talent for getting things done and in smoothing over objections. Two glimpses of Caiaphas in action *before* Christ's trial are provided in John (7:46-53; 11:45-53), which should disabuse us of any notion that he was only a figurehead. Caiaphas' reasoning powers were evident in the Court's deliberations following the raising of Lazarus.

It would be unfair to Caiaphas to consider him the deputy or dupe of Annas. He was more the skilled facilitator than the conceiver and innovator of daring policies. Caiaphas was 'a wily manager of men; a master of assemblies with a fitting gift of speech'.[5]

Pomposity and prestige did not prevent the presiding chief justice from secretly cringing before Jesus, the lowly carpenter. But Caiaphas effectively hid his trepidation, although deep down he was frightened by Jesus. Caiaphas was in command of himself and of the assembly. He could articulate and be persuasive in his discussion of alternatives as to what to do with Him.

Caiaphas' talents in dealing with the Romans, who made sure there were many turnovers in the high priest position (they appointed them), are well-documented. Some diplomacy (or was it bribery?) had to be behind his nineteen year term.[6] In addition, Caiaphas was able to walk a thin line with the Pharisaic members in the Sanhedrin when he convinced the Pharisees to let stand the political charges against Jesus (Luke 22:1-3).

Caiaphas showed a consistent disdain towards our Lord. Caiaphas was curt and contemptuous. Once Caiaphas' mind was made up, he was impatient with technical details that would slow his ambitions (Matt. 26:65 – 'What need we of further witnesses?'). His callousness towards Jesus was similar to when Judas was rebuffed in returning the betrayal money (Matt. 27:4-6). Caiaphas not only had a low view of Jesus, he had previously shown he had a low view of his colleagues. A toxic trace of disdain for others was evident in his sweeping statement: 'you know nothing at all' (John 11:49). Caiaphas had a high opinion of himself.

Near the end of Jesus' trial before Caiaphas, Caiaphas abjured Jesus to confess or deny, under oath, whether he was the Messiah and Son of God. Unashamedly Jesus disclosed His identity, and at that point Caiaphas dramatized his irritation by standing up and tearing his robes. In what seemed almost mid-sentence, Jesus was met with the histrionics of the prestigious chief justice.

The Rending of Caiaphas' Clothes

If we tear our clothes, it is usually by accident. Caiaphas, however, tore his on purpose and, as he did, said, 'He has spoken blasphemy!' (Matt. 26:65).

Had Caiaphas improvised a theatrical turn? Had he resorted to a pretentious show? Was it his own idea and was it proper? Surprisingly, the code of high priest's conduct allowed for such an act. Only in special cases and under extreme conditions was a high priest permitted by law to do such. According to Leviticus 10:6 and 21:10, the high priest was not allowed to tear his clothes even in grief over the death of a spouse.[7]

> The fact that there was no relaxation of this rule, even for a near relative, shows how strict were the regulations.[8]

The wording of Mark 14:63, in the parallel account, indicates that he tore to his *under*clothes.[9] That probably meant the tearing was violent rather than indicating that Caiaphas had great muscular strength.

Since the meeting was probably held in Caiaphas' home, rather than the Hall of Hewn Stone, where the official high priest robes were housed,[10] surely what Caiaphas wore that night was not the official robe.[11] At any rate, whether the tearing was done for effect or was a spontaneous expression of horror,[12] it hardly proved blasphemy.

The really shocking part of what transpired was not what Caiaphas did to himself, but what he did to Jesus. It was not that Caiaphas lacked judicial decorum, but that in judicial practice he resorted to symbolic showmanship, possibly pretending that he complied with judicial law.

Caiaphas' upset over Jesus' alleged blasphemy was a subconscious attempt at misdirection, of getting the members to focus upon what Jesus claimed rather than what he, as chief justice, was doing. (What Caiaphas had done should have made him put on sackcloth and sprinkle ashes!)

Caiaphas had not lost control of his emotions. Nor had he postured for effect (although both possibilities have been entertained by students of the trials). Rather Caiaphas had a complete disregard for truth and justice.

> The veil of truth is rent, too, by priestly hands,
> That hides divinity from mortal eyes;
> And all the mysteries to faith proposed,
> Insulted and traduced, are cast aside, as useless.[13]

The Rending of Truth

The real tragedy was Caiaphas' commitment to get rid of Jesus before the proceedings began. He had previously announced in the Sanhedrin that it was necessary for Jesus to die (John 11:50).

Tailors would be aghast at making ribbons of expensive judicial-priestly robes, but what was most upsetting to lovers of truth was Caiaphas' determination to achieve his aims in disregard of justice.

Some would say, 'Hold on a second! Those who were judges on the Great Sanhedrin got there, in part, because of their integrity. Would a chief justice be capable of such a thing? Was it likely?'

One feature of Ellis Rivkin's presentation on Jesus' trials was that the evil actions attributed to the Sanhedrin on religious grounds were unthinkable.[14] One of his starting points was the non-punitive disposition of the judges, i.e. their basic benevolence. But such an assumption does not fit the first century Gospels.

Certainly it is unwarranted to make the same assumption about courts today, especially after the disclosure of the inner workings of our Supreme Court. From no less an insider to the Supreme Court, the late justice William O. Douglas, who retired in 1975, comes an admission that personal prejudices seeped into decisions. It was not the Constitution alone which determined where they came out. As an example of this, Justice Douglas cited the faults of his former colleague, Justice Felix Frankfurter, which he considered fairly typical, who decided cases without creating a hedge against predilections, personal loyalties, political preferences, and dislikes.[15]

Ancient jurists found resistance to the tug of preference equally difficult. Caiaphas' performance was dictated by a power play to preserve the *status quo* in Judaism, in which he played a principal part.

Obviously Caiaphas was eager to condemn Jesus. Proof of this came when Jesus said, 'In the future you will see the Son of Man sitting at the right hand of the Mighty One and coming on the clouds of heaven' (Matt 26:64, NIV). Caiaphas interrupted with the declaration 'Blasphemy! You have heard the blasphemy.'

The Charge of Blasphemy

But what was blasphemy? Caiaphas altered the definition for his peers and they played into his hands. Blasphemy was to say something against God. It was to make arrogant statements against the Law.

> According to the rabbis, every one who spoke disrespectfully of the Torah or 'stretched his hand to God' could be regarded as a blasphemer. Several incidents in the history of Jesus and the apostles show that the broader interpretation was current at the time of Jesus.[16]

But Jesus did not do that.[17] Indeed, from the Christian viewpoint, Jesus spoke the truth. Even from a Jewish viewpoint He spoke the truth, for it was no blasphemy for anyone to declare he was the Messiah. Jesus was only asserting His true loyalty and rightful intentions. It was Caiaphas who construed it as 'blasphemy'.

Caiaphas, not Jesus, engaged in blasphemy, for Caiaphas spoke against God in accusing Jesus of blasphemy, for Jesus was God, not just Messiah. Thus, Jesus was charged falsely. And the truly guilty party, Caiaphas, received no condemnation. It causes one to consider who was really judge and who was really criminal. Self-deception drove Caiaphas deeper into denunciation and allowed him the dubious luxury of self-justification.

How serious was the court's charge of blasphemy? For when the Sanhedrin finally remanded Jesus to Pilate, they never brought up the blasphemy charge! (See Luke 23:2 and the next chapter on Pilate.)

> Why do we need any more witnesses? Look, now you have heard the blasphemy. What do you think? (Matt. 26:65, 66, NIV).

Nothing in the witness phase of the trial more clearly showed that justice itself was shredded and that Caiaphas used the blasphemy charge as a pretext for having Jesus executed. Steps were skipped in the legal process so that what resulted was a kangaroo court in which rules were dropped and rights denied.

Most notable was that Caiaphas had violated judicial sequence. Jesus was provided no legal counsel, to start with, and Caiaphas squelched testimony on Jesus' behalf. In capital cases the trial must open with reasons for acquittal (The tractate, 'Sanhedrin,' *Mishnah*, 4:1). Proofs of evidence must precede.[18] For Caiaphas such a beginning was inadmissible.

Witnesses in Court

Witnesses were crucial in Jewish court cases. Without them there was no trial. The witnesses' testimonies constituted the charge. Until heard there was no accusation or indictment. The agreed testimony of two witnesses (Deut. 17:6) constituted both the evidence and the indictment.[19] Cross-examination of the accused could not take place until after two witnesses agreed. If the prosecution failed to make a *prima facie* case, there was no right to question the accused. 'The judge was not entitled to make up for the shortcomings of the prosecution by questioning of the accused.'[20]

The Sanhedrin had a tough time trying to dredge up two testimonies which agreed. Much delay was encountered in finding testimonies which could satisfy the prosecution (Matt. 26:59, 60). Formal agreement between the witnesses was more important than what actually was said or done (*Mishnah* 'Sanhedrin,' 5:2).

The two allegedly agreeing testimonies were hardly indisputable. One person testified that Jesus said, 'I will destroy' (Mark 14:58 [verse 59 makes it seem this was different from the Matthean citation which follows]) which did not agree with two who testified that Jesus said, 'I am able to destroy' (Matt. 26:61). Between these two versions there was no real agreement. Moreover, the Gospel of John has preserved the actual wording of Jesus when He first cleansed the Temple in the first week of His ministry. (On the matter of one or two Temple cleansings, see Appendix 2.). He actually said:

Destroy this temple, and I will raise it again in three days (2:19, NIV).

Corroboration that Jesus was a Temple smasher could be built on what was said. Jesus was referring to officials in Judaism as destroying His body. It was His destroyed body that He would raise. As it turned out, all the fuss about Jesus' alleged plans to demolish the Temple was unfounded. What actually happened, of course, was that the very ones who said He would destroy the Temple turned out to be the cause for which the Temple was destroyed (ironically fulfilling the judicial pattern noted in Psalms 7:15, 16; 9:15, 16 and in Proverbs 26:27).

The worst construction one could place on the faulty testimonies would be that they showed:

sacrilege for the Temple ('will destroy') or
sorcery ('able to destroy')

One further confirmation that Caiaphas ignored justice is the fact that the accused could not be condemned on the basis of his own testimony. The famous Jewish jurist Maimonides said:

Our law condemns no one to death upon his own confession.[21]

Jesus' Silence

Our Lord stood silent when Caiaphas tried to provoke Him to respond (Matthew 26:62 – 'Are you not going to answer [the witnesses]?').

Wait a minute, before you blindly agree with the judge. Had the witnesses agreed? In fact, they gave inconsistent testimony. They hadn't agreed. They were inconsistent. Caiaphas was in such a hurry to conclude the session with a conviction he didn't take serious notice of the discrepancies in the various testimonies. For Jesus to engage in self-defence would have been superfluous and 'would have implied self-incrimination'.[22] Caiaphas had egged Jesus on to defend Himself. But that was in violation of established Jewish judicial practice.

Mistreatment of truth led eventually to mistreatment of person. Jesus was struck in the face by members of the Sanhedrin. Cruelty followed injustice.

[Caiaphas] was as fixed as the ice of an Arctic winter, as unresponsive as the dead.[23]

Caiaphas had participated in the brutality. He not only encouraged but he participated in Jesus' physical abuse. He engaged in spitting upon Jesus, slapping, blindfolding, and striking Jesus with fists (Matt. 26:67, 68).

Everyone laughed: How could Jesus know the future when He couldn't identify His assailants (Matt. 26:67, 68)? In their minds, Jesus was a fraud and that apparently excused their abuse of Jesus, or it freed them to think they would not be accountable for their truculent brutality.

What should not be overlooked is the fact that the Roman soldiers were not the only ones who beat up Jesus. Later, they spat upon Him, also, as 'a parody of the kiss of homage customary in the East'.[24] But in this trial the Hebrew justices took part in mocking and brutalising Jesus. How grossly was Jesus abused! Terrible enmity against the Son of God burst forth in animalistic action under the pretence of legality in Caiaphas' court.

Sarcasm and sadism had taken over the Great Sanhedrin. They wouldn't think of spitting on Caiaphas' floor, but they thought nothing of spitting in Jesus' face! What took place after they called for his condemnation was not innocent horseplay, but a hate-inspired baiting of the Lion of the tribe of Judah. The members who first rejoiced in misrepresenting Him, last took delight in mishandling Him.

The Rending of the Heavens

Yet a note of triumph rang forth in that foul atmosphere. In our Lord's announcement of the convening of the Heavenly Court, the grimness which accompanied their malice was pierced with the cutting laser light of His truth.

> But I say to all of you: in the future you will see the Son of Man sitting at the right hand of the Mighty One and coming on the clouds of heaven. (Matt. 26:64, NIV)

Jesus had alluded to the Old Testament. Indeed, Jesus conflated two texts: Daniel 7:13 and Psalm 110:1. Jesus said in effect, 'If you want witnesses, then hear two from the Old Testament. What you ignored, I will cite, and what *they* have to say agrees without straining.'

The Sanhedrin was going to be overruled by the Highest Court of all. In God's time Jesus was to restore justice. He would split the Heavens and disrupt the nature they have abused in tranquillity. Then, all who would not acknowledge His Lordship will witness a cataclysmic rending of natural law and share a colossal reformulation of earth's elements.

Little did they realise that Jesus, who would restore nature in grand style, could easily have wrecked them in their ambition to annihilate Him. Unlike the Sanhedrin, which was unbending as petrified trees, nature would respond to Him with a unanimous and undeniable affirmation that He was both Messiah and God. *It* would show what *they*, in their hostility and unbelief, would not confess.

> Day of anger, day of wonder,
> When the world shall roll asunder,
> Quenched in fire and smoke and thunder,
> O, vast terror, wild heart-rending,
> Of the hour when earth is ending,
> And her jealous judge descending.[25]

Which was easier, to tell who smote Him or to tell how many hairs were on their corporate heads? Which was easier, to give the names of His mockers, or to tell when the cock would crow the third time at Peter's denial? Which was easier, to identify His assailants or to tell who would betray Him?[26]

The flexing of Jesus' justice was ahead. The planets would vary their orbits to make way for their Master. Angels would converge to watch in wonder.

Christ's ability to rend the Heavens was hinted at and given as a perpetual reminder to them and to us, when the Veil of the Temple, which was four inches thick, which teams of horses could not tear, was rent the day Christ died.

God tore down the curtain separating the holy place from the holy of holies in the Temple, which was a real and symbolic invitation for all persons to enter Heaven's courts through Christ's torn body.

What motivates us to enter His courts? Seeking the Lord for His own worth, rather than for our benefit, propels worship ahead of the major motivation in idolatry. Self-serving satisfaction, from which we cannot be completely delivered, runs the risk of reducing God to a convenience. Our point of contact with the Lord causes warped thoughts of our own purity to recede.

Our encounter with God, of course, does not make Christ's return less important or unnecessary. Rather, it makes it more glorious. *Our* entrance into His presence, by the gift of grace and God's mercy, becomes the moment of *His* entrance into our lives. Christ is in the business of banishing mental constructs which bear little resemblance to His image. Therefore, we greet His reigning power as a welcomed event long before His final, forceful, majestic return.

We must not wait to know God as Judge. We should know Him today as Saviour. Christ is present in the Scriptures. It is there that we meet Him best. It is the biblical Christ who leads us to the Father's throne. Since Christ has opened a new and living way, let us come before Him in praise and prayer. It is a marvellous privilege and irrevocable blessing.

To enter His presence now, or better, to have His presence enter us, takes away any fear of meeting God later, when Christ asserts, unfurls and applies His glory at His second coming.

CHAPTER 4

CHRIST BEFORE
PONTIUS PILATE

[28]Then the Jews led Jesus from Caiaphas to the palace of the Roman governor. By now it was early morning, and to avoid ceremonial uncleanness the Jews did not enter the palace; they wanted to be able to eat the Passover. [29]So Pilate came out to them and asked, 'What charges are you bringing against this man?'

[30] 'If he were not a criminal,' they replied, 'we would not have handed him over to you.'

[31]Pilate said, 'Take him yourselves and judge him by your own law.'

'But we have no right to execute anyone,' the Jews objected. [32]This happened so that the words Jesus had spoken indicating the kind of death he was going to die would be fulfilled.

[33]Pilate then went back inside the palace, summoned Jesus and asked him, 'Are you the king of the Jews?'

[34] 'Is that your own idea,' Jesus asked, 'or did others talk to you about me?'

[35] 'Am I a Jew?' Pilate replied. 'It was your people and your chief priests who handed you over to me. What is it you have done?'

[36] Jesus said, 'My kingdom is not of this world. If it were, my servants would fight to prevent my arrest by the Jews. But now my kingdom is from another place.'

[37] 'You are a king, then!' said Pilate.

Jesus answered, 'You are right in saying I am a king. In fact, for this reason I was born, and for this I came into the world, to testify to the truth. Everyone on the side of truth listens to me.'

[38] 'What is truth?' Pilate asked. With this he went out again to the Jews and said, 'I find no basis for a charge against him.'

See also Matthew 27:2, 11-14; Mark 15:1-5; Luke 23:1-5.

Suspense quick-freezes time. This is especially true of mysteries. And it is true in trials, where guilt is at issue. But once the facts are out and the trial is finished the suspense is gone. In this respect, Christ's trials miss some of the suspense in trials currently going on. The motivation of Jesus' opponents was never in doubt. And the final outcome was soon fact. From the perspective of the New Testament nothing was more certain than *who* wished Jesus dead and *how* Jesus finally died.

Surprises

Yet as Christ's trials progressed there were many surprises. The surprises came both in what tactics Jesus' opponents used and Jesus' response to them. From the start Jesus was never surprised. One cannot dismiss this feature as exclusively Johannine, for the Synoptic Gospels show the same. He knew what was developing, if not exactly how and when the ordeal would intensify and climax. Jesus took time to forewarn and prepare His disciples of His early death (Mark 9:30-32; 10:33). Though Jesus had told His disciples not to be surprised (John 13:18, 19, 21), they were probably still unable to both anticipate the pending events and their predisposition to weakness under pressure.

The Sanhedrin was certainly surprised when one of the twelve volunteered to hand Jesus over to them safely under cover of darkness (Mark 14:10, 11). Their elation with this windfall far exceeded the meagre amount they gave to Judas for his co-operation. There must have been surprise laced with chagrin or maddening frustration when they could not find damaging and agreeing witnesses against Jesus (Matt. 26:59, 60).

That there was an explosive ending to Jesus' short career was no surprise. The more Jesus spoke, and the more he did, the deeper he became in trouble with the religious authorities. His unpopularity escalated swiftly in Jerusalem, the capital and centre of Sanhedrin influence. Even in the northern areas where the popular party of the Pharisees had substantial impact Jesus encountered mounting criticism, which he tried to calm and lessen by avoiding premature confrontations in Galilee's population centres (Mark 1:45). Jesus' exhortation after healing would frequently be to tell no one.[1]

Jesus' Withdrawals

In the main, Galilee was sympathetic to Jesus' ministry, but even there He had to withdraw to avoid premature capture. Mark records four withdrawals from Galilee (6:30-53; 7:24-30; 7:31–8:10; 8:27–9:30). If one chooses to consider withdrawals from towns, then there were ten (6:31, 32; 6:45, 53; 7:24; 7:31; 8:10; 8:23; 8:27; 9:2; 9:30, 33; 10:1).[2] Jesus withdrew to prevent a precipitous termination of His work.

That Jesus could no longer avoid a showdown became evident after three years of intense itinerant mission. That Satan had his day in the arrest, trial, and death was expected by Jesus, but, in the light of Jesus' predictions and warnings, was foolishly unexpected by the disciples.

How the scenario of Jesus' holocaust developed was surprising. No area had more surprise than the phase from the Sanhedrin trial(s) to the civil trials.

The modern reader of the Gospels, so conditioned by television, may miss being able to visualize the physical sites involved in Christ's trials. The exact places are open to question.[3] More important than logistics was the logic of what was done and why. We should place the matters of motivation above the matters of material settings.

Certain transitional questions arise concerning Jesus' appearance before Pilate. Three major ones arise. Questions

1 and 3 are related more to Israel's spiritual condition, which occasioned the enigmas. Question 2 is more of a technical nature, which we have chosen to answer in the Appendix 1: Legal Questions:

1. Why was it necessary to forward Jesus to Pilate and have a Roman trial, since Jesus was declared guilty of the capital offence of blasphemy?

2. In view of the fact that the Sanhedrin knew that Rome had deprived them of the right of taking a life (John 18:31), wouldn't it have been simpler, faster, and more diplomatic to go straight to Pilate and avoid convening court on the eve of Passover?

3. Why was the charge of blasphemy, the alleged previous conviction before Caiaphas, dropped once Jesus was before the Roman court? The Sanhedrin concluded their examination of Jesus on the angry note of blasphemy. But the Sanhedrin recognized the verdict of blasphemy had no real punch with Pilate.

'Something's Rotten' in the System

Jesus' critics in the Jewish hierarchy were feeling their way along in trying to have Jesus done away with legally, swiftly, and without a finger of suspicion pointing at them. What drove them to declare Jesus guilty of a capital offense boiled down to their own malice and vengeance, two emotional components which forced them to seek and secure Jesus' elimination.

Also involved was the larger question of the resurgence of Israel's unfaithfulness to God. The abuse Jesus suffered was a clear sign that unbelief was a natural reaction even of religious persons. Hence the Sanhedrin epitomized opposition to the Incarnate Word of God. In the Old Testament there are repeated stories of spiritual defection from the Lord. Israel's leaders apostatized. Its practices were polluted with polytheistic additions. But when Jesus lived, everyone thought its inclinations for corruption were past problems. Israel's worship was pure, its leaders untainted with evil, its commitment to Scripture complete, its ideals intact. These were all appearances, however, for

> Just then, under the sway of this victorious monotheism, Israel's Messiah was handed over by Israel to the Gentiles and nailed by them to the cross with Israel's approval. Could there be a better proof that this monotheism is not a final achievement and expression of Israel's obedience to the first commandment?[4]

Corruption and weakness combined in the Sanhedrin's efforts to get rid of Jesus. At this juncture their goal was in sight. Jesus' end was near. They sensed it. But there was also tentativeness and trepidation. The task was not complete. Several obstacles were in their way. These were legal rather than spiritual. What should have bothered them didn't. Instead of being concerned about violating their ceremonial prescriptions in touching Gentile property (John 18:28), they should have been horrified by the desire to take Jesus' life.

> [The Sanhedrin, which represented the world-spirit] has made its decision against the revelation and wants to be rid of the man who disturbs its peace. It cannot do it of itself; it cannot silence his word through its own word; and since the means at its disposal are ineffective against His superiority, it appeals for help to the authority of the state; the world [i.e. the Sanhedrin] acknowledges that the state is over it, but it misuses it for its own purposes, exactly as it misuses for its purposes its religious law.[5]

The Sanhedrinists were desperate to keep their image intact and to eliminate Jesus. They saw the Roman governor as their solution. It was easier for them to remand Jesus to Pilate than for them to repent of their wrong doing and restore Jesus to Israel. It was their spiritual separation from God which finalized their decision to see through His separation from Israel. Their basic motivation was hostility toward the revelation they professed to want.

Warnings about Religion

Despite the Sanhedrin's sophistication and success we are clearly warned that such achievements in religion are detrimental to serving God, for they make the ego so self-satisfied that any challenge to that centrality will meet determined opposition. Also, the inference is present in these events that claims to piety because of performance are likely to be hollow.

No more relevant lesson emerges from Christ's trials than that religion is more a cloak to hide from the true God than an ambitious undertaking to find God. It is a substitution for God rather than a reliance on God. To miss this truth is to have missed the major point of Christ's passion.

Of the four judges who tried Jesus, Pilate is the judge best known. He gets mentioned every week around the world, wherever Christians recite the Apostles' Creed: 'Suffered under Pontius Pilate.'

Pilate, Jesus' Best Known Judge

Pilate entered the office of Procurator, also called Prefect, four years prior to Jesus' trials. Emperor Tiberius had appointed him in AD 26 as the fifth governor of troublesome Judea. That in itself was a surprise, since Pilate was outspokenly anti-Semitic.[6]

Pilate was appointed to govern Jews, and like all Roman politicians his distrust of them has the appearance of hate. Avoidance of difficulties would be unlikely.

61

[Pilate] was ill adapted for the government of a race so tenacious of its faith and so quick to resent whatever seemed a slight upon its cherished traditions.[7]

Good Romans were found among the Idumeans (Herod Antipas) and Jews (the Apostle Paul). It is incorrect that only Italians could be Romans. Seneca, from Spain, became a famous Roman. Yet in hindsight Pilate was almost as bad a choice to govern Judea as it would be to elect a Klu Klux Klan member as chief of security for the NAACP. On the other hand, Pilate proved to have some capability of working with Jews, for his administration tenure (26 to 36) was longer than most.

Several incidents prior to Pilate's trial of Jesus made toeing a just line difficult. Rome's openness to Jews becoming Romans and rulers would not have prevented Pilate from being racist. The Passion narratives suggest to me that racism clouded Pilate's perceptions. By a twist of divine providence, Pilate sarcastically titled Jesus 'King of the Jews', a title which the chief priests both deplored and tried to have changed.

A quick review of three conflicting incidents may be sufficient to show Pilate's poor prior relationship with his Jewish subjects. These clashes added to the tension of the trial. First, he showed bad judgment in electing to advertise his Romanism in Herod's palace. It had the effect of waving a red flag in front of a Spanish bull.

Pilate erected votive tablets/shields bearing the name of Emperor Tiberius in the Palace of Herod. Pilate thought it within his rights to erect these patriotic symbols in his quarters.[8] But people took offence. Criticisms soon grew into angry denunciation. Even Herod Antipas and his family jumped into the controversy. Pilate scorned the objections of prominent Jewish landowners, i.e., specifically the Sanhedrin who, backed by the sons of Herod, sent a delegation to Rome and appealed to Tiberius. Pilate was ordered to remove the offensive tablets. (These were placed in the Temple of Augustus, Caesarea, where the year-round praetorium was).[9]

Pilate was not only the chief military officer; he was in charge of province finances.[10] Indeed, the title 'procurator' stressed the financial aspect of his rule, whereas the earlier 'prefect' emphasized the military character of the post.[11] A solvent province was a well managed province. Therefore, Pilate looked after taxation of the populace.

Pilate's Management of Judea

For taxation purposes the province was divided into eleven taxation districts.[12] Judea could not expect to run on the imperial treasury (*fiscus*), so it had to have its own public treasury (*aerarium*).[13] The Romans had a tax on land (*tributum soli*), a general tax, including imports (*vectigalia*) (Matt. 22:15-22), and a head tax (*tributum capitis*) (Luke 2:1-3). Roman taxes were a sore point with most Jews.[14]

It was the funding of Judea which occasioned another major run-in with the Jews. Pilate angered the citizens by misappropriation of funds.

Cash flow was a definite problem in public projects, such as in the construction of a new city water supply system in Jerusalem. When money ran out, or to supplement the existing treasury, Pilate took large amounts of Temple funds. That was met with vociferous objections, for encroachment into the sacred money stores raised the hackles of every self-respecting Jew. What happened was not going to slide by, for the public was aroused.

Pilate's Handling of Civil Disturbances

Pilate got wind of the planned uproar in the streets, so he dispatched military personnel in disguise among the protesters. When the pitch of shouting began to indicate loss of control, on signal, the 'secret police' brought out clubs from beneath their robes and dispersed the crowd. Josephus told of many being killed.[15]

Covert action against the state terrorists was an area where Pilate came off looking bad. Luke recorded an unprovoked massacre of Galileans in the midst of offering sacrifices in the forecourt of the Temple (13:1ff), probably on the eve of the second Passover when Jesus was not in the city (cf. John 6:4). They were probably rebels or Zealots, whose hatred for Roman occupation fired Jewish loyalists. The ambush slaying of Zealots was conceived as a fear tactic, but it backfired. Instead of branding the movement unpopular, it placed an aura of martyrdom upon their cause.

These incidents indicated bad blood between Pilate and the populace. What he did as military commander and as financial officer affected his performance as judge. His record in the military and taxation departments influenced his decisions as judge. His past rose up to affect the future; Pilate's record in one department influenced his decisions in another.

Judea was one of the most difficult provinces to handle. It was a third class imperial province. This troublesome province provided many tense moments. The Passover season was a nightmare for Pilate. The troops were on alert to put down trouble at a moment's notice. Each time Pilate returned to Jerusalem, memories of his former confrontations undoubtedly came back to haunt him. At least yearly, Pilate visited the hotbed of Judaism, Jerusalem. Trouble was most likely to erupt during Passover.

Pilate's Role as Judge

Pilate's third responsibility as governor was judge. The trial he was most famous for conducting was initially viewed as a nuisance case, although as time bore out, it became the most notorious criminal case of human history.

Jesus was taken to Pilate at dawn, which was the time he preferred to hear cases. That dawn was the eve of Passover.

The usual procedure was for the accused and his accusers to enter the praetorium for the trial. (In Roman practice the governor of the province was the judge, jury, and executioner in one).[16] But the Jews refused to enter, lest they invalidate the lengthy purification preparations and precautions they had fastidiously performed. Unless they stayed clear of Gentile property they would be unable to celebrate the Passover meal that afternoon. Therefore, they refused to enter the praetorium (John 18:28).[17]

The Dynamics of Contacting Pilate

Their insistence on avoiding contact with Gentile property on the eve of the Passover had missed the Old Testament emphasis that cleansing from defilement was an inward state shown outwardly. The outward was to represent the inward.

In time the outward measures replaced, rather than reflected, the inner state. Inward cleansing was what was needed by man, but conscience was eased by compliance with rules, largely ceremonial. They would not overstep their desire for proximity and 'pollute' themselves. Therefore, they were careful not to rub against the praetorium walls.

That didn't bother their consciences, but stepping over a ritual line did. What kind of piety was it that would make them careful to stay 'pure' from Gentile property, yet indulge in the sinfulness of desiring Jesus' life unjustly? They were concerned about their enjoyment of the Paschal lamb immediately after sunset, but they were not concerned about the final Paschal Lamb, the only Lamb that could cleanse.

At Passover God reminded them of His faithfulness to the nation, but as a court they were punishing Jesus for His faithfulness. More tragically, they saw no injustice in demanding an innocent man's death. They ended by shrieking for Christ's execution. Another demonic inconsistency was their condemnation of Jesus because He did not meet their expectations of being a military messiah, yet they sought His death because He was an alleged nationalistic messiah figure.

They hoped that Jesus' appearance, when taken to Pilate, would be enough to convince Pilate that He was a criminal. He was brought bound. He showed marks of having been beaten. The implication was that He was guilty. But Pilate was not going to be forced to rubber-stamp their opinion. His contempt for Jews and his own self-respect would not allow that.

Roman Trials

Roman trials were designed to be public. Pilate's presence out of doors didn't make the trial less valid. There was a spot for the *bema* already. For Jesus to be tried in the outdoors was not Pilate's concession to their scruples. But for Jesus to enter with Pilate was no concern for them, because they had no intention of giving the accused one last request – of eating 'an anticipated Passover meal' (R. T. France). They considered Him defiled and not worthy of protection. (Of course, Jesus had anticipated what was coming, so He had celebrated the Passover before His arrest.) Pilate had his judgment chair, the *bema* brought out into the open, and the inquiry of Jesus' accusers proceeded.

Pilate asked, 'What charges have been brought with the prisoner?' (John 18:29).

The Sanhedrinists first attempted to have Pilate avoid a new trial. This is indicated by their opening:

If he were not a criminal, we would not have handed him over to you (John 18:30, NIV).

By his question, Pilate was letting them know that a new trial was beginning and that he was not going to validate their accusations without a thorough investigation. Pilate had decided to try the case as a new one, although – possibly for convenience sake – he could have exercised his right to accept their accusations as final.[18]

Pilate would not accept generalized guilt. Moreover, even if they found Him guilty of violations of Jewish Law, such as blasphemy, they still needed to go to Pilate to allow them to stone Him. Apparently, in the full quorum meeting of the Great Sanhedrin, the possibility of having Pilate approve their stoning of Jesus was discussed. That was apparently their first choice. Stoning was their first option. But even for that they would have to approach Pilate. On second thought, they dismissed stoning, for that would mean they would execute Jesus. They decided to formally present the charge of sedition or crimes against the state, which was never brought up during Christ's appearance before Caiaphas the night before. This would mean that Pilate would do their dirty work.

Pilate forced them to specify their charges. He was not going to agree the condemnation without a new trial. If Jesus could have been guilty of a non-capital crime, their coming to him would be a total waste. They didn't want Him fined; they wanted Him finished!

In Jesus' trial, it became plain that Pilate was on trial. As a mockery of Pilate's sole judgeship in the proceedings, Pilate unwittingly stood before three courts not of his own choosing.

Pilate before the Bar of the People
Although Pilate exercised his authority to try Jesus as a new case, he was under no illusion about Jewish respect for his court. Their request for Pilate to validate what they previously decided meant that they considered an examination by Pilate

superfluous; yet at the same time, they realized they could not get around Pilate. To try to keep their hands clean they knew they had to go through Pilate. In a real sense they were before Pilate's bar.

Yet, Pilate could not luxuriate in that position, without having the feeling that he was under their thumbs because of his own previous excesses. He had irritated the populace. Surely, he had proven that he was over them, but in exerting his authority he placed himself at a disadvantage at a crucial moment when he wanted to act free of any encumbrance.

Forcing his critics to petition Caesar to take down the tablets had put Pilate in a bad light. Confiscation of sacred money and the unprovoked assault of citizens protesting their grievance over the misappropriation of Temple funds to complete a capital improvement project put him in the position of *needing* to come up with a concession to improve his image.

Pilate gave an unqualified, automatic 'No!' to their surly demand to validate their verdict. Either he acted as if he did not know that he had the right to agree with them, which would make Pilate look totally incompetent concerning the rights that went with the *imperium* (least likely), or else he gave the impression that Jesus was guilty of a lesser offence and therefore would not warrant a state trial.[19]

Pilate was being hounded by a mysterious power of the subjects he considered to be dirt. Surely, before the bar of the people he stood condemned, hands down, unless he came out with a conviction of Jesus.

So as it turned out, Pilate's past haunted him. Pilate's cruelty, greed, stubbornness, deceit and theft were factors which contributed to the mix of giving in to the outraged constituents. Admit to it or not, his previous deeds would come back to wreck him. (But we must not get ahead). At this point, however, Pilate seemed unaffected by thoughts about past acts. He would admit to his acts, but he would acknowledge no wrong. How Pilate reacted in the end game indicated that he was likely to bow to their pressures.

Pilate began looking strong, at first, but the longer the trial went on the more he showed signs of giving in to their authority. What contributed to Pilate's bending to the will of the people could possibly be the fact that his patron Sejanus had fallen out of favour.[20] Pilate eventually knuckled under to the demands of the crowd. He did not want to sacrifice his position by refusing to grant their demand. At their insistence Pilate handed over Jesus to be crucified.

Pilate before the Bar of Conscience

Outside the biblical record Pilate has been described as 'unbending, ruthless' – so wrote Herod Agrippa I to Emperor Caligula.[21] If the evaluations of Josephus and Philo (two Jewish writers soon after the time) were to be accepted without qualification, then Pilate was a rat.

It would be wrong to picture the Four Gospels as exonerating the Romans, although there seemed to be less surprise and outrage against their role, as Josef Blinzler has noted. Yet, one of the great ironies of the Gospel records is that underneath the brutality and racial bigotry of Pilate there were a few cracks in the facade of power, cracks through which a wedge for truth could have been made.

Pilate showed some sensitivity, if not morality. Though Jesus' Jewishness was a hurdle for Pilate's appreciation, he did sense Christ's greatness. Jesus showed a commanding presence, a penetrating intellect, and a disarming peaceableness which impressed Pilate to the point that he genuinely did not see the need to have Him destroyed. For Pilate to declare three times that charges against Jesus were *groundless* (John 18:38b; 19:4, 6) and then end up ordering His crucifixion revealed he was driven by self-preservation rather than by principle.

Paul wrote later that Jesus witnessed a good confession before Pilate (1 Tim. 6:13). Jesus' non-combative yet affirmative answers; His absence of hostility toward His captors, accusers, retainers, and judge; and His affirmation of Kingship as being non-political, together convinced Pilate that Jesus was being framed.

The chief obstacle to Pilate's sticking by justice was his racism. Pilate had a repugnance for Jews. He asked, 'Am *I* a *Jew*?' (John 18:35). Pilate was not a closet anti-semite. Through both segments of the trial, it seems Pilate was contemptuous of Jews. His last order was anti-Jewish, for, against the protests of the priests, Pilate insisted on retaining the title 'King of the Jews' (John 19:22) in order to mock his manipulators.

What a bundle of contradictions! Seemingly sympathetic toward Jesus, yet holding Jews, of which Jesus was one, in utter and complete contempt. Pilate's conscience was schizoid: at one point, he leaned toward justice, yet at another point he bent away from freeing one Jew, Jesus of Nazareth.

Pilate had experienced a vague sense of truth in Jesus. Despite his dismissal of truth in his contemptuous question – 'What is truth?' (John 18:38) – he encountered a resilience in Jesus, which was one truth which lay strangely on his mind.

But the bottom line for Pilate was that he was to remain a pagan in whom self-trust and seasoned bigotry would prevail, which not even conscience could mollify, overcome, or expel.

Pilate before the Bar of Truth

Pilate took Jesus inside the praetorium to closely interrogate the accused. Pilate refused to approve the indistinct verdict of Jesus being guilty of death without specific charges being filed. Luke 23:2 mentions the threefold charge brought against Jesus (look at the text), all three of which were state related, and one punishable by death. It was upon those accusations that Pilate's interrogation was based.

The definition for 'King' meant one thing to the Jews and another for a Roman. For Pilate a kingdom had to have borders. A King had to have soldiers, and his soldiers had to have had weapons. For a foreign King to be in another's territory meant a threatened takeover. But Jesus disabused Pilate of these elements.

Jesus did not deny, but affirmed that He was truly king (John 18:37): 'You are right in saying I am a king.' Jesus went on to qualify the type of kingdom He led. His kingdom was mediatorial, not military. Jesus said:

> My kingdom is not of this world. If it were, my servants would fight to prevent my arrest by the Jews. But now my kingdom is from another place (John 18:36, NIV).

Pilate's ears were unfamiliar with such talk of kings without objectives of forced conquest and of a kingdom without violent expansionist plans. Jesus wanted truth, not political action. Jesus said He was king of the realm of truth:

> I was born ... into the world, to testify to the truth. Everyone on the side of truth listens to me (John 18:37, NIV).

Pilate's Preliminary Position

Jesus' type of Kingdom was to be extended by teaching, not by force. His borders were to be enlarged, not by taking from, but by adding to. A non-temporal kingdom made no sense to Pilate. At this point, Pilate injected the question: 'What is truth?' (18:38)

Some may see in this Pilate's despair of ever finding truth, perhaps gesturing to the noisy crowd outside. Or, as the majority rightfully conclude, he asked it with an air of cynicism, possibly turning to pick up a goblet or a gavel, or drumming his fingers in disgust. Whatever the tone or whichever the gesture, Pilate did not wait for Jesus' answer but went out again to the crowd.

Pilate's gravest mistake was in not waiting for an answer. He turned away from Jesus to pronounce his opinion on Jesus' innocence. Ironically, Pilate left to utter a truth, the truth of Jesus' guiltlessness. No better starting point could have been used in the search of truth. He left to speak the truth: 'I find no basis for a charge against Him' (18:38b, NIV).

Pilate left off in his investigation of Jesus. He would have done better to quiz Jesus more thoroughly about His concepts, to inquire diligently about the truths Pilate could not discover on his own. In this impatience with hearing Jesus out, Pilate is a warning to modern man.

Pilate's neglect of giving a patient hearing to Christ is a warning to moderns that the pursuit of truth on a personal basis with Christ is wise beyond words. No other quest can match it. No other object can rival it.

Pilate flashes a warning signal in the moral darkness of our times. Ultimate questions, cosmic issues, deserve our attention. Christ's truth is an expansive realm, roomy and ranging. It is a tragedy not to explore it and not to engage in personal investigation. The Bible is Christ's domain. We are losing out not to be intense students of the Scriptures which teem with life and pleasures.

Pilate at this phase of the trials should stop us from lowering our sights to lesser goals. We are reminded by Pilate's missed opportunity not to walk away from Christ and see what the waiting crowd wants.

From Pilate's brief interrogation of Jesus he had gathered the truth of Jesus' innocence. That is a truth worth cherishing, defending, and glorying in.[22] In recent times it has been considered valueless. But the lost world needs to hear more than that.

The truth which is one step beyond Christ's innocence is His righteousness. The positiveness of Jesus' perfection sums up the essence of God's salvation for humanity. The truth of Christ's righteousness given to unrighteous persons forms the core of the Good News. It is this we need to study. It is this we need to search. It is this truth we need to share. From Christ's own lips we must learn the glorious Gospel.

Our society is hope-starved. The glorious righteousness given to unworthy sinners is the hope we hold out to a despairing world. Only in lingering with Christ can we learn from Christ. And only in absorption of God's self-revealed truths is there salvation. But receptivity is vital. If Pilate had been in less of a hurry, if he had been humble, not proud, if he had not been controlled by hatred of Jews, if he had been willing to bite the bullet of Jewish rejection, instead of incurring divine rejection, then the personal destiny of Pilate would have been different.

Pilate scorned the truth, yet he indirectly confirmed the truth that we make openness to the Gospel less likely when our minds are rusted shut with accumulated hang-ups and a backlog of misdeeds. We must be made open to all that Christ, as Truth, has to impart. Our persons are locked up to sin until we are freed by the power of the Holy Spirit.

> Will God impart His light
> To them that ask it?
> Freely – 'tis His joy, His glory and His nature,
> To impart,
> But to the proud, uncandid, insincere,
> or negligent enquirer –
> Not a spark![23]

CHAPTER 5

CHRIST BEFORE
HEROD ANTIPAS

Luke 23:6-12

⁶On hearing this, Pilate asked if the man was a Galilean. ⁷When he learned that Jesus was under Herod's jurisdiction, he sent him to Herod, who was also in Jerusalem at that time.

⁸When Herod saw Jesus, he was greatly pleased, because for a long time he had been wanting to see him. From what he had heard about him, he hoped to see him perform some miracle. ⁹He plied him with many questions, but Jesus gave him no answer. ¹⁰The chief priests and the teachers of the law were standing there, vehemently accusing him. ¹¹Then Herod and his soldiers ridiculed and mocked him. Dressing him in an elegant robe, they sent him back to Pilate. ¹²That day Herod and Pilate became friends – before this they had been enemies.

Pilate met an impasse in Jesus' first appearance before him. He had pronounced Jesus innocent (John 18:38). But this did not sit well with the Sanhedrinist accusers of Jesus. It aroused them to restate their charges with more vigour and vehemence. Luke preserves their words:

> He stirs up the people, teaching all over Judea, starting from Galilee, even as far as this place (Luke 23:5, NASB) .

A desire for Jesus' conviction was deep. Their feelings about Jesus' alleged guilt seemed too strong to dissuade.

Pilate's Predicament

Pilate had previously encountered Jewish determination. He knew they were fully skilled to skirt, shun, and scuddle any barriers raised to spare Jesus from death. From former bitter experiences Pilate knew that Jewish fanatics could not be cooled or even channelled. Therefore, he wished to get rid of this troublesome case by one means or another.

'GALILEE' – Pilate thought, 'That's my way out! Here is a technicality in the nick of time. I don't have to continue trying Jesus. Jesus is from Galilee and the ruler of Galilee, Herod Antipas is in town .... He should try the case!'

Who was Herod Antipas? How did he fit into the rulership scheme of Palestine? Was he, like Pilate, also Roman? Unless we get a perspective of Herod Antipas' position and refer to his past, it will be hard to come to grips with his distinctiveness. Therefore, we need to consider some background matters.

Brief Historical Review

First, we need to step back and briefly review Rome's involvement in Judea in the first century. Who rules? Jesus lived under two Caesars. Christ was born under Emperor

Augustus Caesar (63 BC–14 AD) and was crucified in the reign of Tiberius Caesar (14 AD).

Israel's occupation by Rome began when it was taken by the Roman general Pompey. Before Augustus' reign Julius Caesar (100–44 BC) reorganized the Judean territory.

In 47 BC, Julius Caesar had put the grandfather of Herod Antipas (whose name he bore abbreviated), Antipater, in charge of all Judea. Judea was a third class imperial province of Rome.[1] 'Prefects' or 'procurators' were put in charge of smaller possessions, and 'legatees', such as Publius Sulpicius Quirinius, were put in charge of the larger country of Syria.[2] Lovers of the Christmas story in Luke 2:1-5 will recall that Quirinius oversaw the census implementation. One of his last acts in office was to appoint the high priest, Annas.[3]

Antipater's son was Herod the Great (37–4 BC), the ruler who tried to exterminate baby Jesus (Matt. 2:1-23). Ruling for Augustus was the Idumean ruler, Herod the Great. Originally Herod had to flee Judea and go to Rome to escape a sentence of the Jewish Sanhedrin, and when at Rome he picked up the confirmation of the Roman Senate as 'King of the Jews'.[4]

When Herod the Great died, Archelaus succeeded him in the province of Judea (Matt. 2:22). Antipas ruled Galilee and Perea and Philip ruled Gaulanitis.

Antipas, Herod's second son, (4 BC – 39 AD), was put into power as part of a settlement among the rival heirs of Herod in 4 BC.

Antipas' Jewishness

Antipas, like his grandfather and father, was Idumean. He was not Roman, though he ruled for Rome. When his grandfather ruled Israel for Rome he was a vassal king or tributary sovereign. When Herod the Great's realm was split up after his death, Antipas was called a 'tetrarch' by Augustus, who appointed him (Matt. 14:1; Luke 3:1). He was also called 'King' (Mark 6:14), although the title was used broadly, not strictly. By this time, the title 'king' was used for any tributary rulers of provinces.[5]

'Idumea?' 'Idumeans?' Even those who have read the Bible may have missed Idumea. 'Who ever heard of Idumea and how does that relate to being Jewish?'

Idumea was the Greco-Roman name for Edom, whose territory stretched far beyond that of ancient Edom. In the time of Jeremiah the prophet (587 BC) Idumea stretched as far north as Hebron (which was south of Bethlehem), as far east as the Nabatean kingdom, and as far south as Beersheba. In 126 BC Idumea was conquered by John Hyrcanus and was Judaized. In Roman times Idumeans were loosely Jews with strong Roman leanings.[6] Josephus, for instance, dubbed Herod the Great 'a half Jew'.[7]

The late Samuel Sandmel described Herod the Great's Jewish connection as follows:

> Herod was a Jew, but not Jewish .... To a limited extent, therefore, Herod was reconciled to an external practice of Judaism, but never with mind or heart or soul.[8]

Herod Antipas was a hybrid Jew. He had a Samaritan mother,[9] and his father had him trained by a famous Jewish orator in Rome.[10] As tetrarch, Antipas worked for Rome. Yet he kept close ties with Judaism.

Several other pieces of information indicate Antipas' nominal Judaism. He sided with the Jewish protesters when Pilate had the votive shields/tablets erected in the Palace of Herod. Coins in his region did not carry the image of Caesar, just the emperor's name. (In this he was more Jewish than his brother, Philip, whose coins carried both the name and image of Caesar).[11] The New Testament shows Herod Antipas fascinated by the Essene-like preacher, John the Baptist (Mark 6:14ff).

Antipas conformed to some elements in Judaism, especially the feasts. It was significant that he was at the Passover at which Jesus was crucified (Luke 23:7). Herod Antipas' territory was not Judea, but Galilee and Perea. It seems probable that he was in Jerusalem at Passover as a pilgrim.[12]

Pilate and Antipas

Pilate didn't let his dislike for Herod Antipas stall him in transferring Jesus to him. 'Perhaps,' he may have thought, 'this may be a way to clear up the bad blood between us.' Two factors probably figured in their feud. First, Antipas strongly objected to Pilate's desecration of the palace of Herod the Great with pictures of the Emperor. Antipas and his sons sided with the Jewish protesters and leading landowners. On top of this Pilate had inflicted harm on the subjects of Antipas, when he approved of the slaughter of the Galileans as they worshipped (Luke 13:1ff).

Herod Antipas felt good that Pilate sent Jesus to him, for it was well-known that Antipas wanted to meet, hear, and see Jesus in operation (Luke 9:9; 23:8). Pilate, who had angered Antipas in the previous Passover, appeased him in Passover AD 33 by transferring Jesus to him for trial. It was a diplomatic courtesy as well as a legal loophole of escaping responsibility for judging Jesus. Luke 23:12 (NIV) reads:

> That day Herod and Pilate became friends – before this they had been enemies.

As in Jesus' hearing before Annas, Jesus' trial before Antipas wasn't really a legal examination. It did not get beyond Antipas' curiosity with Jesus. There was no judicial inquiry, just personal inquisitiveness and mockery.

Only Luke recorded this trial. Why? Probably because the primary recipient would have special interest in this neglected feature. It seems probable that Luke dedicated his Gospel to a high Roman official, who had taken on a Christian name 'Theophilus'.[13] Perhaps the mysterious Theophilus had some acquaintance with Antipas.

> Theophilus, who as probably a Roman officer, would have been deeply interested in the relationship of the Herods with the prefects of Judea.[14]

When historians wonder what value this episode has in terms of trial, one answer is that it was another indication of Jesus' innocence of the charges. Another worthy point was regarding the base motives of Antipas in dealing with Jesus. It is to this we turn next.

Profile of Antipas

Antipas' style gives us a glimpse of the substance of his character. What was Antipas like? How he conducted himself before Jesus shows he fits into the glimpses elsewhere in the Gospels.

One such glimpse of Herod Antipas comes from his birthday party attended by notables (Mark 6). Herod Antipas' deficiencies were apparent. In Mark 6 Herod Antipas celebrated his birthday with his friends. There he appeared vain, audacious, self-serving, boastful, and self-indulgent. In an intoxicated state he rashly promised anything to Salome, whose sensual dance aroused in him erotic feelings. In Luke 23, we see him in a more formal setting, and more in possession of his wits. There he appears as a person interested in Jesus as an entertainer.

It was as if the charges brought against Jesus only cluttered Antipas' desire to hear Jesus speak and see Him perform. He mostly wanted a private audience with Him. When Jesus' accusers hurled accusations at Him, Herod showed no interest in the charges. As far as he was concerned, nothing of what was said warranted the death penalty. Herod wanted to focus on ideology and Jesus' itinerary, rather than pursue His alleged insurrectionist activities. Antipas didn't follow through in extracting more detailed information on the charges brought against Him, apparently ignoring them.[15] Luke 23:8 and 9 (NIV) says:

> From what he had heard about [Jesus], [Antipas] hoped to see him perform some miracle. He plied him with many questions, but Jesus gave him no answer.

Antipas, like his father, was successful in new construction and building programs. He oversaw the erection of three cities.[16] His realm was divided into two areas and each of these was divided into five *toparchies,* which were again sub-divided. One of the *toparchies* (Betharamphtha or Julias) was comprised of fourteen villages. Antipas had some organizational talent and goal-setting ambitions.

Alexander Whyte deprived Antipas of managerial achievements:

> Herod Antipas was more of a circus-master, than a serious-minded monarch.[17]

Nevertheless, the fashion-plate, fun-loving monarch was clearly there. Antipas was more in line with a playboy prince than a sociopathic ruler or bumbling bureaucrat.

> We must picture the prince, not as a sinister inquisitor, but rather as a capricious, jovial and affable person.[18]

The flawed Rock-opera *Jesus Christ Superstar* presented controversial interpretations of Jesus and those around Him. While the dialogue was fabricated, I believe, in one instance, something of the appropriate tone was caught and conveyed in the depiction of Herod Antipas. What it had him say fitted Antipas perfectly.

Jesus I am overjoyed to meet you face to face. You've been getting quite a name all around the place. Healing cripples, raising the dead. And now I understand you're God, at least that's what you've said. So you are the Christ, the great Jesus Christ... Prove to me that you're divine, change my water into wine. That's all you need to do and I'll know it's all true. Come on, 'King of the Jews!' So if you are the Christ, yes, the great Jesus Christ, feed my household with this bread, you can do it on your head ... Come on, 'King of the Jews!'

Herod Antipas sat back, draped in his shining white robe and Jesus stood in His blood-spotted rags. Jesus looked soiled, more like a common derelict rather than a sensational healer.

Antipas' Superficial Expectations
Antipas wanted to be entertained; excited yet detached. Antipas wanted Jesus to dazzle him with feats of His power.

It is entirely in the character of the frivolous prince that he is interested in Jesus primarily as a wonder-worker, and seems to forget completely why He had been brought before him.[19]

Antipas was not seriously interested in testing Jesus' claims, nor in trying His case. Antipas wanted to be stimulated and see a spectacular show of power. Final proof of this was Antipas' reaction to Jesus' refusal to speak or act.

Antipas' love of luxury was evident in the way he dressed.

He was never declared 'king' by Caesar, but he liked to play the part and be called 'king' though he was not.

His robe was described as bright white. The expression means glistening (ἐσθῆτα λαμπρὰν – Luke 23:11). It is not the expression used for the purple cape of the Roman soldiers (John 19:2, ἱμάτιον πορφυροῦν). The 'gorgeous robe' of Herod Antipas is not to be confused with the common-place military red cape of the Roman soldiers used in the mockery scene in the last phase of Christ's trial before Pilate (John 19:2).[20] Herod's robe was undoubtedly white or silver, a garment that glistened. Agrippa I, who followed his uncle Antipas, wore a shining robe in Acts 12:21.[21] White was worn by kings and by those who were candidates for office (*toga candida*).[22]

Antipas did not engage in the brutality of the earlier and later mockers, who punched, slapped, and whipped Jesus. He didn't strike Jesus. He insulted Jesus when Jesus refused to co-operate in performing a miracle. Jesus' silence both galled and amused him. A scene of mockery took over when Jesus showed persistent silence.

When the evangelist tells us that Herod and his soldiers treated Jesus with contempt and mockery, one can well imagine that the tetrarch did this by giving the signal for general laughter with some mocking or scornful words. It is very probable that he compared his own position with that claimed by Jesus and cried, in mock astonishment: 'So you're a king, are you? Well, you have gotten farther than I have.'[23]

It would be a dramatic moment of his own devising if Antipas would enter the mocking circle and raise the pitch of witticism by taking off his own robe and sarcastically placing it around Jesus, saying, 'Which are you, candidate for royalty or incumbent?'

Herod Antipas' love for flair and finery is missed if we

imagine him dressed in heavy purple and not in light white. Thus, Jesus not only stood mocked in the dirty, cast-off, red officer's cape from the barrack's laundry pile, but also he stood mocked in the expensive and elaborate white robe of Antipas!

With that form of mockery, the disdainful jest on Jesus' kingship could continue into the Praetorium of Pilate, for Pilate would have immediately recognized the robe as Antipas'. He would accept Antipas' dressing of Jesus as an expression of his new goodwill, and also a signal to Pilate that Antipas did not consider charges against Jesus as having any substance. In his own mind, apparently, Antipas didn't see that Pilate could escape final responsibility, or, what may be more likely, Herod Antipas did not consider Jesus guilty. In sending Jesus back to Pilate, Antipas indicated that Jesus was innocent and not dangerous.[24] So Pilate's expectations were fulfilled.

It is almost certain that Pilate expected the tetrarch to acquit Jesus.[25]

Antipas considered Jesus lacklustre, a travelling preacher in need of some polish and pizzaz. (As if glitz and glory were the same.) Antipas did not anticipate that God chose to put His glory in the plain Jesus. He, the very revelation of the glory of God, appeared ordinary (John 1:14).

Antipas' Judaism, as we have seen, centred on externals. His main interest was in festivals and finery, for outward things, and for the unusual.

Religious Entertainment

Religion interested Antipas to the degree it could entertain. He was not interested in truth. Jesus had just finished telling Pilate that He was King of the realm of truth and that His followers were willing to explore that with Him. And then He was faced with a person (unlike Pilate), who professed to have an interest in Jewish truths. But, instead, Antipas was occupied with pious fluff and show biz stuff.

Antipas' attitude is still alive. It has infected countless 'Christians'. How many go to church to be entertained would be hard to calculate. But, surely, there is a significant number who prefer few words and a lot of action. To attract and keep the crowds some clergy are willing to throw in theatrics and melodramatics. Otherwise, it is felt that interest will lag and attention will drag. Showmanship is considered good growth strategy. Popular tastes crave stimulation.

A plain Jesus is considered drab, unappealing, deplorable. As Antipas thought Judaism's wardrobe was threadbare and dull (else why would he like to listen to John the Baptist?), so modern churchmen look to the church for safe amusement and sanctimonious celebrations.

What occupied the early Christians? What were they seeking? What did they look for in Christianity? Notice, when it all began they were not impressed with expensive and elegant buildings, whether of glass or of stone. The church of the *Acts* had no splendid buildings, no luxurious accommodations, no gorgeous sanctuaries. They met in homes and in the open air. Their primary focus was upon understanding the Gospel and in sharing it.

New Testament Plainness

As Jesus stood unadorned before Antipas, so He continues to appear in the pages of the New Testament to the modern man. What Jesus said is not enough, some think. Antipas-like people feel compelled to supplement Christianity with elements that often turn out to divert attention away from its original splendour.

Jesus' physical appearance contrasted with that of Antipas. Jesus wore a seamless undergarment (John 19:23), the only expensive piece of clothing ever attributed to Him. (But that could not be seen!)

More than likely, God thought it appropriate for the true, final High Priest, Jesus Himself, to wear what the official state High Priest, Caiaphas, himself wore in compliance with Jewish custom.[26] But at this time, all that Antipas could see of Jesus' wardrobe was simple and inexpensive, and dirtied by abusive attendants.

A robe of lies was placed on Jesus. The Sanhedrinists heaped on Jesus derision more demonic than Antipas' frivolity. They covered Him over with base lies. The tampering Sanhedrinists tried to tack lies to Jesus. They interjected their derogatory comments all the way through, even when Jesus was suspended on the cross (cf. their taunts in Matt. 27:40-42, 49).

The Sanhedrinists had spun and spewed all kinds of half-truths and outright lies to make Jesus look bad in the eyes of the populace, whose interest He had caught. Disinformation was draped upon Jesus from the inception of His ministry and all the way through to His exodus. The chief priests who had accompanied Jesus to Antipas, who were present accusing Him, did this as a cover-up of the real royalty of Jesus, which they found distasteful.

Antipas bombarded Jesus with questions. But Jesus stood alone, silent. Antipas viewed Jesus' silence as personal defiance, rather than contempt of court, for in Antipas' mind it was not truly a court session. Other men could crawl on their knees for Antipas' favours and do his bidding, but Christ would not dignify Antipas' worldliness and his insensitivity to truth.

Silent Response from Jesus

In His silence before Antipas Jesus made a statement. He was 'saying' something still relevant for our times. Christ still says nothing to the person who seeks Him as a diversion. Antipas represented those today who primarily seek a spectacular experience. Certain church attendees leave services impoverished because they dismiss any gospel intellection with the slur that it is 'intellectualism'. And that snobbery in regard to substance is a by-product of having made theatrical sensationalism their preference and priority. Christians should not expect concentration on words in an anti-intellectual atmosphere. Words bore those who seek stimulation without thought. Since the Scriptures are words, focus on the biblical text is difficult for a significant number of people. Even God's words cannot avoid the abstract. They describe the intangibles. And that becomes an obstacle.

Should we develop extensive ceremonial actions in worship with fewer words? Enthusiasm for conceptual concentration has fallen on hard times. Worship specialists advise more congregational participation that makes no mental demands. Intellectual content has been considered detrimental. But do emotional outbursts ever reach the level of honouring God, as is done by a rich vocabulary sincerely expressed?

Malcolm Muggeridge's complaint about secular disparagement of words is worth citing:

> One of the things that appals me and saddens me about the world today is the condition of words. Words can be polluted even more dramatically and drastically than rivers and land and sea.[27]

Along with pollution of words comes the dilution of the Word of God. Listeners should decry the paucity of Scripture in sermons.

Jesus refused to play games with Antipas. Christ continues to say nothing to the persons who are absorbed in sensationalism. Christ continues to say nothing to the person who has given up on words. And if our main interest in Christianity is its accidental and seasonal pageantry, then Christ cannot show Himself in sustained, meaningful ways.

Another reason why Jesus said nothing to Antipas was Antipas' shallow interest in the real Jesus. Antipas would only turn for serious consideration to something unusual. Thus, Jesus' silence was one way He showed that Antipas was insensitive to His nature.

Antipas, in a sense, kept repeating his attitude to authenticated prophets. Recall what Antipas had done to John. Then Antipas only had a superficial interest in the preaching of John the Baptizer. Recollection of Antipas' inability to take prophets seriously must have passed through Jesus' mind, as well as the memory of John's execution to satisfy the hateful whim of Herodias.

Memories of John the Baptizer

John was precious in Jesus' sight (cf. the encomium of Matt. 11:8-11). For Herod to carry through the evil wish of Herodias was inexcusable. Antipas' alleged interest in John's preaching was superficial, because he had no moral courage to refuse to destroy an esteemed servant of the Gospel.

Antipas showed no contriteness in having John the Baptist destroyed. Antipas evidenced callousness despite the comedy he tried to create. He felt no need to seek Jesus' forgiveness. It was not just the idle threats which made Jesus stand silent, but the previous insensitivity to the life of John.

Too Much Talk, Not Enough Listening

A final factor which kept Christ quiet before Antipas was the fact that Herod Antipas talked too much. He importuned Jesus with a flood of words (Luke 23:9).

The problem was not that Antipas was uninterested in words because he sought Jesus to perform miracles. In one sense, words dominated Antipas. He was not averse to words. He used them. But they were all *his* words.

We cannot hear the Scripture when we seek for reassurance and confirmation of what we bring to the Bible. When we are filled with our own opinions, we are unable to adopt God's. When we are spiritually deaf God says nothing. To closed minds Scripture is silent. A person closed to God finds Christ mute. Surely God has spoken in the Bible, but the words of God cannot be truly heard in faith when our minds are controlled by our pre-occupying conclusions.

Missing out on Hearing God

Antipas missed Jesus' greatness as God, because he was mastered by an entertainment mood. Antipas made demands on Jesus. He would set the agenda for Christ. He tried to call the shots. He wanted Jesus to conform to his idea of what a Messiah would do.

The bottom line as to why Antipas missed the hidden glory of Christ was because he was so taken up with his own importance. Antipas wanted the dazzle of fools' gold. By extracting that he would avoid the true brilliance of Christ. Antipas didn't want to worship Christ. He only wanted to watch Him. Jesus, however, was unco-operative to Antipas' approach. Antipas never thought his approach was wrong, but that Jesus was wrong. Herod Antipas judged Jesus innocent but odd, clever but cold, harmless yet stubborn. To him Jesus was not to be feared, but to be made fun of. Antipas grossly misjudged Jesus.

We would distance ourselves from Herod Antipas in his faults. Few today would engage in Antipas' cruel mockery before transferring Jesus back to Pilate. We recognize Antipas' action as patently impolite, professionally rude, and judicially felonious.

Herod Antipas' fault was to glide on the surface of rarefied religion, content with thrills. He was not really interested in the substance of who Jesus was or what He came to do. He was drawn to Jesus only because He made and kept religion interesting.

Have people ceased duplicating Antipas' attitude of ruling out the need for exposure to God's Word? Do we have pre-cut patterns of conformity for Jesus to fit? Do we, like Antipas, seek Jesus for curiosity's sake?

Herod Antipas concluded that Jesus could not deliver. When Antipas sent Jesus back to Pilate, it took the form as much of banishment as of legal behaviour. The way he punished Jesus for refusing to put on a show was to send him back to Pilate. Similarly, we would dismiss the real, the historic Christ of Scriptures when He does not conform to us and cater to our ideals. Churchgoers are in danger of repeating Antipas' faults.

Seasoned Christians can fall prey to Antipas' fault of approaching God with a life of expectations. Jesus continues to reserve the right to do nothing and to say nothing to us. Jesus' silence before Herod was a symbol of our unanswered prayers. To tell Jesus to write our script borders on Antipas' presumption.

Reconciling ourselves to an unknown future designed by our Lord is difficult. Our obligation is to accept the only Jesus there is, the One in the New Testament. *That* Jesus was vocal and final. Some, to their own hurt, would prefer the Jesus Herod Antipas met, the Jesus who doesn't speak so they can have the last word. But He who hears every idle word will apply in words that prior Word given in the Scripture, when He begins the final judgment.

CHAPTER 6

CHRIST BEFORE
PONTIUS PILATE
(Final Appearance)

³⁹ 'But it is your custom for me to release to you one prisoner at the time of the Passover. Do you want me to release "the king of the Jews"?'

⁴⁰They shouted back, 'No, not him! Give us Barabbas!' Now Barabbas had taken part in a rebellion.

¹Then Pilate took Jesus and had him flogged. ²The soldiers twisted together a crown of thorns and put it on his head. They clothed him in a purple robe ³and went up to him again and again, saying, 'Hail, king of the Jews!' And they struck him in the face.

⁴Once more Pilate came out and said to the Jews, 'Look, I am bringing him out to you to let you know that I find no basis for a charge against him.' ⁵When Jesus came out wearing the crown of thorns and the purple robe, Pilate said to them, 'Here is the man!'

⁶As soon as the chief priests and their officials saw him, they shouted, 'Crucify! Crucify!'

But Pilate answered, 'You take him and crucify him. As for me, I find no basis for a charge against him.'

⁷The Jews insisted, 'We have a law, and according to that law he must die, because he claimed to be the Son of God.'

⁸When Pilate heard this, he was even more afraid, ⁹and he went back inside the palace. 'Where do you come from?' he asked Jesus, but Jesus gave him no answer. ¹⁰ 'Do you refuse to speak to me?' Pilate said. 'Don't you realize I have power either to free you or to crucify you?'

¹¹Jesus answered, 'You would have no power over me if it were not given to you from above. Therefore the one who handed me over to you is guilty of a greater sin.'

¹²From then on, Pilate tried to set Jesus free, but the Jews kept shouting, 'If you let this man go, you are no friend of Caesar. Anyone who claims to be a king opposes Caesar.'

¹³When Pilate heard this, he brought Jesus out and sat down on the judge's seat at a place known as the Stone Pavement (which in Aramaic is Gabbatha). ¹⁴It was the day of Preparation of Passover Week, about the sixth hour.

'Here is your king,' Pilate said to the Jews.

¹⁵But they shouted, 'Take him away! Take him away! Crucify him!'

'Shall I crucify your king?' Pilate asked.

'We have no king but Caesar,' the chief priests answered.

¹⁶Finally Pilate handed him over to them to be crucified.

See also Matthew 27:15-32; Mark 15:6-19; Luke 23:13-26.

The Gospel of John has two significant trial omissions. First, the trial before Caiaphas is omitted. Also, it doesn't have Christ's appearance before Herod Antipas. But much space is devoted to the Roman trials by Pilate. *The Gospel of John* gives the most complete picture of Pontius Pilate in the Gospels.

The Contribution of John

Despite these omissions we are indebted to the writer of the Fourth Gospel for three principal features not found in the others. These include the private conversations between Pilate and Jesus, the unwillingness of Jesus' accusers to enter Pilate's property, which necessitated his going out to Jesus' accusers, and the scourging/mockery scene in the *middle* of the last trial rather than the one just prior to sending Him off to be crucified.

Some are less concerned about these differences than they are with the overall presentation of Pilate. Pilate, they contend, is portrayed sympathetically. The impression is that Pilate was favourable to Jesus, wanting to spare his life. The evangelist, however, marks the Sanhedrinists to be villains. Pilate's weak attempt at seeking to acquit Jesus, to many, made him look well-meaning. Again, the question of the historical reliability of the Johannine account is raised.

Time in John

The chronology of John's Gospel has attracted special interest for a number of reasons. His chronological references differ from the Synoptics. Although John uses general time phrases, such as 'early morning' (18:28), the concluding point of the final trial is more specific – 'about the sixth hour' (19:14). This time-frame varies from the Synoptics. It differs in other particulars, as well, such as in the fact that in John the Passover proper had not yet been commenced when Christ first appeared before Pilate, because they didn't want to be disqualified from the Passover meal (18:28). This would mean, therefore, that Jesus and His disciples ate the Passover meal (chapter 13) earlier.[1] J. H. Bernard concluded:

> The Fourth Gospel seems to have been constructed on a rough chronological plan more precise than appears in the Synoptics.[2]

Study of chronological differences will help us understand the peculiar styles and aims of the Synoptics and that of John. The details are too many to discuss here. Outside reading on chronological questions is necessary for a grasp of the arguments for the various theories.[3]

A theology of time stands out in John. The Fourth Gospel makes theological dynamics its main focus. Chronology, as such, was only incidental to the theological purpose of the Gospel. It was not just the number and variety of Jerusalem feasts Jesus attended, but the significance of the events He faced. Beside the prism of the dawn of eternal life (God's qualitative life now for those committing themselves to Christ), there is the stress on the prism of the 'hour', which has a predestination overtone.[4]

Apart from Jesus, in John's Gospel no one else was concerned about God's clock. The Sanhedrinists were concerned to finish Jesus so they could begin their Passover celebrations. To the Sadducees especially, there was no divine co-ordination of anything, let alone Jesus' death. The timing of what happened as fulfilment of Old Testament prophecies about the Lamb of God meant much to the author of the Fourth Gospel (cf. 19:24, 32, 33, 36).

Jesus, a Legal 'Hot Potato'

Pilate wanted to get rid of the case and not spend any more time on it. Not even Pilate could alter time. The clock was moving swiftly and the case was becoming more complicated. He discovered that each expedient he used to slip away from it was frustrated.

Pilate tried several ways to get away from dealing with Jesus' case. He first tried to have Herod Antipas try Jesus. No mention of this is in John's account of the trials. There is no break in Jesus' appearance before Pilate. But the most likely place for the trip to Herod Antipas was probably John 18:38.[5]

But that did not work, for Herod sent Jesus back to Pilate. The transferral only postponed Pilate's having to face Jesus again; it did not avoid the second meeting. The administrative move brought Pilate some satisfaction. It helped him mend a break between himself and Herod. When Herod returned Jesus there was a momentary pleasure in Pilate that nit-picking Antipas was of the same persuasion as Pilate, i.e., that Jesus was innocent of the crime of sedition.

Pilate resorted to a second expedient in trying to let Jesus go free. He used the Passover amnesty choice (Matt. 27:15-26; Mark 15:1-16; Luke 23:13-25; John 18:39, 40).

Amnesty?

According to Roman practice there were two types of amnesty: *abolitio*, which was the freeing of the prisoner *before* sentencing, and *indulgentia*, which was freeing *after* sentencing. It seems that Pilate felt he was offering Jesus freedom at the choice of the crowd *before* sentencing and that they took it as the offer to free *after* sentencing.[6]

C. H. Dodd suggested that Pilate's willingness to let the crowd decide on Jesus' fate was due to his deep dislike for the Priests. It may have been his attempt to snub the Sanhedrinists, by ignoring their direction and playing to the grandstand.[7]

Pilate felt no constraint from time, except that he couldn't get rid of it fast enough. The main pressure he felt came first from the Sanhedrinists and finally from the Passover mob. Crowds were his concern. Pilate had to deal with three kinds of crowds.

The crowd under Pilate

The crowd under Pilate were soldiers, hundreds of them. They were described as a cohort, which numbered between 600 and 1,000 soldiers. The Judean wing of the Roman army were really auxiliary soldiers.[8] They were trained and experienced military, though recruited regionally. Riot control was their primary responsibility, but they also had special duties such as scourging and crucifixions.

The Alternative of Scourging

The third attempt to mollify the clamouring multitude, who wanted Jesus destroyed, was Pilate's decision to have Jesus scourged.

There were two types of beatings prescribed by law:

1. *Fustees*, which was a light beating for those, for instance, who started a fire inadvertently.

2. *Flagella*, or the severe scourge.[9]

It was the *Flagella* which was the beating ordered for Christ. The Jews beat with rods or the three-thonged lash, but the Romans used the nine-thonged and bone-studded whip. The painfulness of the punishment has not been sufficiently told in our time.

But the horror of the Roman scourge is hard, historical fact. The Romans put no limits on the number of strokes and with several soldiers taking turns it meant a severity unlawful in Judaism. The tool was the cat-o-nine-tails. It was made of a stick with leather thongs. Each strand had a stone or jagged piece of metal fixed to the free ends. The victim was tied to a post. In this way the back was stretched so that the maximum area was exposed. The cuts were deep, exposing the body to infection. Some descriptions tell of flesh hanging in shreds. 'The veins and sometimes the very entrails were laid bare.'[10] Its brutality caused many to expire. Jesus' early death from crucifixion was probably due to the severity of the scourge to which Pilate subjected Him.

The scourge was cowardly and cumulative. It was cowardly because the tormentors did not have to look upon the face of the victim. (It is easier to hurt someone when you don't have to face them. That is why gossip is done 'behind one's back'!)

The torture was also cumulative. The first blows hurt badly, but the subsequent ones stung even worse. Each succeeding blow intensified the pain. New wounds crisscrossed the old and suffering increased with each stroke.

Lacerations on the face-side of our bodies we can see and treat. But wounds to the back are unreachable and not seen; felt but untreated. This partly explains why this suffering was difficult to deal with. It would require care from someone else, and Pilate would allow none for Jesus.

Pilate foolishly hoped the scourging of Jesus would satisfy the crowd's desire to see Jesus suffer. After all, he may have thought, these are pilgrims seeking mercy for themselves from God; perhaps they will seek justice, love mercy, and walk humbly with their God. He naively thought that the Jewish audience would say Jesus had been punished enough and call for Pilate to set Him free.

The crowd over Pilate

Jerusalem was packed full of people for Passover. In addition to the total Jerusalem population (inside and outside the wall), estimated to be around 30,000 people, there were the pilgrims. Including the pilgrims, the total population inside the walls during Passover, therefore, would have swollen to be between 60–80,000.[11] Even at the lower figure, the space was extremely tight.

Enormous crowds strained every facility. Quarters were more than close. A large percentage of the pilgrims camped outside the city.[12] Roads were snarled in traffic. Movement was slow. Getting through took a long time. Street vendors were happy, but security forces were overworked. The Romans had their hands full.

Crowd control was a real problem. The size of the Passover pilgrim population was staggering and unwieldy. Quarters were cramped, and accommodations were strained. Any public uproar would have been disastrous.

Of course, the vastness of the Passover population contributed to the excitement of the festival. But for Pilate it only contributed to his exasperation.

Crowds have their psychology. Multitudes have their own mind. Intelligence seems to be over-ridden by instinct in masses. Rollo May noted:

> Man's most effective way of evading the daimonic is by losing himself in the herd. This conformism and anonymity relieve us of the burden of responsibility for our own daimonic urge, while insuring their satisfaction.[13]

The baser instincts of man come forth in group demonstrations and large rallies. There is a sense of hiding behind the larger groups, which frees the angry to express emotions, whereas when one-on-one they would be passive or polite.

Why would Pilate be willing to follow the crowd and comply with their inconsiderate demands? Certainly, he showed himself to be a non-philosopher in walking away from Jesus when he asked, either in despair or sceptically, 'What is truth?' (John 18:38). If Pilate were a utilitarian in philosophy he would feel confident in going with the proposition, 'the greatest good for the greatest number'. But there is little likelihood that Pilate anticipated, embraced, or advocated utilitarianism as a philosophy.

Politicians cannot survive, even when appointed by a centralist figure, unless they pay attention to their constituents. The Pharisees had an eye for large numbers (Mark 11:32; 12:12; 14:2). As the highest body in Judaism's power-structure, the Sanhedrin, also, were keenly aware of how masses had a mind, however unthinking. They wisely hesitated about attempting to arrest Jesus during Passover (Mark 11:18; 12:12; Luke 20:19). Yet, at the same time, the sophisticated leaders detested the ordinary citizen, the 'am ha'aretz'.[14]

Pilate's misplaced hope

Pilate hoped for a streak of pity in the crowd of pilgrims. He initiated the scourge, partly at least, 'to exhaust and to soothe the fury of the Jews'.[15] When Jesus was brought out, Pilate gestured to Jesus who was dressed in a soiled purple cape, with a crown of thorns on his head, thinking that the sentiment of the people would be for leniency, not severity; for release, not for further abuse. He said, 'Behold the man!' (John 19:5)

Various possibilities for this expression are worth considering. In classical Greek, it had the idea of 'the poor man'.[16] Combined with the sight of Jesus smeared with blood and in a weakened state was the clothing of mockery. Perhaps it was Pilate's sick way of trying to convince the crowd that Jesus could not possibly be King – look at the wretch! Pilate may have thought, 'How could anyone seriously think of Him as King of the Jews in a praiseworthy, serious sense?'[17] Pilate was hoping the ghastly sight of Jesus would play on their emotions and become a weight on their consciences. But it didn't have that effect.

The opposite reaction happened. It only served to accelerate their desire to finish the job and destroy Him altogether. Pilate had made a serious miscalculation. Pilate over-rated the crowd's respect for law, and he under-rated the crowd's need for vengeance.

Jesus told Pilate that greater guilt belonged to the person who handed Him over to him. That was not Judas, for Judas turned Jesus over to Annas and Caiaphas, not to Pilate. It was the President of the Sanhedrin, along with its members, who accompanied Jesus to Pilate.

> You would have no power over me if it were not given to you from above. Therefore the one who handed me over to you is guilty of a greater sin (John 19:11, NIV).

Jesus did not deny Pilate's authority, but said it came from God. Nor did Jesus pass off Pilate's involvement, as if he were the victim of circumstances. Pilate was not exonerated. Nor was his guilt lessened. But in terms of the enormity of the crime and sin, Caiaphas bore more responsibility and guilt.

Caiaphas was an evil man, not just an unbelieving man. Pilate's unbelief was less diabolical, less vindictive, more compromising, more compassionate. But both men were indisposed to accept Christ.

Were Jesus' Enemies Evil?

Historians usually avoid commenting on whether participants in human events are moral or immoral, evil or good. Some, nevertheless, expose their own analytical angle of the human psyche, past and present. In the case of Jesus' judges some say they were good men with wrong intentions. Consider the comment of John Marsh, a recent British commentator:

> What the story shows is that the crucifixion of Jesus Christ was not the result of an alliance between men motivated wholly by vicious inclinations; it is rather that good men are driven to evil sometimes by the very soundness of their good intentions.[18]

Had Jesus' judges good intentions? Are not intentions implied in action? Are not attitudes reliably reflected in deeds? If actions show intentions, then clearly their intentions were evil. In John's Gospel, the reference to darkness as the move behind extinguishing the light (1:5)—obviously to snuff it out—affirms that unchanged human nature is controlled by evil within, by a disposition that is evil-dominated and satanically inspired. At first those dominated by darkness retreated from Christ, but then after they regrouped they plotted their counter-offensive. What happened to Christ was not the result of non-malicious oversight, but of a diabolical malevolence which resented the assertive Word of God in the world.

Our Lord emphasized in His conversation with Nicodemas that human nature is intentionally powerless to correct attitudes and behavior opposed to God. No one can self-correct himself or give himself rebirth. Moral transformation must be all of God, the result of the Holy Spirit's action. Flesh cannot raise to the level of spirit (John 3:6). Evil deeds point to evil hearts (John 3:19). Jesus elsewhere taught that only evil men can do evil things (Mark 7:20-21).

In the Gospel of John the hierarchy of human agents

instrumental in Jesus' demise expressed and exercised their evil in ways peculiar to their roles. Caiaphas represented unbelief in the form of spiritual blindness; Judas represented unbelief in the form of personal spite (John 6:70; 13:2, 27), and Pilate represented unbelief in the form of irresolute cowardice (19:12, 13).

To argue that the conclusion of Christ's life on earth was merely the result of well-intentioned misjudgments by otherwise model individuals is to miss the point of the Gospel of John. An easy dismissal of the event of Christ's death as due to good intentions turned sour or due to circumstantial over-reactions, is to miss the true motivations which were in operation. More was involved than tactical miscalculations.

The Cross, God's Probe

Drilling the depths of human nature was one by-product of the cross. In the 1960s, the American Association for the Advancement of Science sponsored a project called 'Mole Hole'. It was a drilling venture in Canada. Every 500 miles, in order to determine the heat variations in the North American continent, the drilling would help determine below the earth's crust the possible makings of earthquakes. The drilling went to 1,800–2,000 feet below the surface to retrieve core samples. God has probed the human heart to record depths. At Golgotha the cross was used to bring out the hostility of man towards God. Man's spiritual temperature was taken at the cross, and the heat levels of hate were enormous.

Pilate's Miscalculation

Pilate's fault was to think that human nature would want Jesus spared and set free. To Pilate the crowd would choose the noble. The crowd was capable of being open, of being reasonable, of shaking themselves free of prejudice. By deferring to the mob Pilate showed a total lack of judgment, a naive presumption of human goodness, and a misguided optimism. He ended placating the rabble rather than following justice.

Pilate represented a Pelagian view of man. What is Pelagianism? And what bearing does it have on the outcome of the trial? Simply put, Pelagianism is the view of man which says man is not born with a sinful nature, that man is a moral neutral, that he only becomes evil when he chooses evil.

To Pilate, talk of evil in human nature was unheard of, preposterous. Pilate stood for being optimistic about human nature. He held to the viewpoint that collective humanity would choose the right. He wouldn't have appealed to them for clemency and compassion otherwise.

The thesis that man is intrinsically good, or that he seeks to please God without any transformation of his being, does not find any support in the closing scenes of Christ's life. The passion stories indeed teach the opposite.

Pelagianism is not an esoteric viewpoint known only by a few, but it is the starting point of all humanity. Everyone starts with the premise that he is all right. It is found in plumbers as well as in professors. A person doesn't have to be a professional philosopher to be Pelagian. Pelagianism has infected the secular understanding of those who have never heard of Pelagius, a fifth century monk who formulated and defended that position.

The Location of Pilate's Court

Where did Pilate conduct court? Two different places are held out as likely locations: the Palace of Herod the Great and the Fortress of Antonia.

The location of the praetorium determined how much space the crowd had for witnessing Pilate's trial outside.

The Fortress of Antonia is the site where, traditionally, the Via Dolorosa begins. It, like the Palace of Herod, had a courtyard. But the courtyard at the Fortress was considerably smaller. The dimensions of the enclosed courtyard at the Antonia Fortress were not on as grand a scale as those of the Palace of Herod. Most scholars reject the Antonia Fortress as the site of Pilate's trial in favour of the site near Herod's palace in the citadel area advocated by P. Benoit.

The size of the outside yard could have affected how many were present to see the mocked Jesus, and how many cried for His crucifixion. William E. Sangster did not think the Fortress of Antonia would hold more than a few hundred. He said, in his estimation, that the space was hardly wider than a street, in which a hundred people would make a multitude.[19]

The crowd was big enough to send up a roaring reaction against Pilate and Jesus. The word used in John 19:6 to describe their screams and shouts is ἐκραύγασαν, from κερυγίζω. The word resembles the raucous cry of a bird of prey. Epictetus used it to describe the croaking of a raven. A raven is a voracious eater with a harsh call.[20]

The crowd under Pilate, that is the soldiers, had strong arms. The crowd over Pilate had strong lungs. They were boisterous. They could boom, 'Crucify, Crucify!'

[The people] were actuated by no real pity, by no zeal for righteousness – they were intent upon their holiday and on their popular rights.[21]

They had cried for Barabbas instead of Jesus earlier. They were in no mood for clemency from Pilate, nor for leniency. They were not satisfied until Jesus was crucified.

According to John 19:6 the crowd was unthinking. The real cheer-leaders of Jesus' demise were the furious chief priests and officials of the Sanhedrin. They were the ones who egged on the crowd, 'Crucify, Crucify!' The crowd was putty in the hands of shrewd handlers of persons. The ones who cheered Jesus on Palm Sunday were the ones who shouted for His death on Good Friday.

The crowd was fiendishly brutal and sought collective safety in their aggressive mood. A call for violent action against Jesus would not easily come forth from the individual citizen or pilgrim. But in a crowd, guilt dissipates and the guilty become faceless. Each person hid behind the other, and thus the terrible cries were collective in their minds, not individual. But those who sin one by one are to be judged one by one.

The herd instinct was running wild. The domino theory was working. The tide against Jesus smashed the hopes of those who were for Him.

But there was yet another crowd Pilate had to deal with.

The crowd in Pilate

He could not see this crowd, but he could feel their pressure. Pilate was full of mixed emotions. Several significant inner 'voices' were being heard. Competing calls shouted in him. There was a crowd *in* him, as well as crowds *under* and *over* him.

One part of his personality called out to spare Jesus. Another faction demanded Jesus' destruction. Three times Pilate voiced Jesus' innocence. He spoke as both judge and witness. The voice of honesty said, 'I find no fault in Him.'

Yet there was the countering voice of prejudice against Jews which forced him not to act on his judicial discernment.

All during the trial Pilate had heard from Jesus' foes that he was guilty of sedition. That was the formally registered charge. But the original accusation voiced against Jesus in the Sanhedrin trial before Caiaphas, in a move patently inconsistent, was used before Pilate the second time around when their frustrations had reached a pitch.

The Jews insisted, 'We have a law, and according to that law he must die, because he claimed to be the son of God.' When Pilate heard this, he was even more afraid, and he went back inside the palace (John 19:7-9, NIV).

A voice of pity came from outside him and became part of the mix. His wife's note – 'Have nothing to do with this just man' (Matt. 27:19) – bore upon him. But the voice from his domestic side was diminutive, lacking decibel strength, compared to the deafening negative voices, which screamed for granting the chief priests and elders their wishes. John 19:12 records: 'Pilate tried to set Jesus free, but the Jews kept shouting, "If you let this man go, you are no friend of Caesar. Anyone who claims to be a king opposes Caesar" ' (NIV).

His wife's voice was shouted down by fear that Tiberius, who had already been annoyed at Pilate's mishandling of the votive shield/tablet flap, would be in no mood to receive another major complaint from the Jews.

In the later part of Tiberius' reign he had become suspicious, gloomy, and temperamental.[22] Pilate stood a good chance of having his position recalled.

Who Was in Charge?

Pilate's supposed neutrality, in actuality, meant that he had lost control. Yet he did not consciously abdicate his responsibility, because in the end he was willing to make a commitment which would seemingly ensure his future. Nevertheless, the voices of justice, of pity, of reason were being drowned out by the voices of fear, of prejudice, and of superstition. His prior offences against his constituents and his personal ambitions were interfering with his performance as a justice.

When claims and counterclaims against Christ are heard, we too are placed in Pilate's predicament.

> Within my earthly temple, there's a crowd;
> There's one of us that's humble, one that's proud;
> There's one who unrepentant, sits and grins;
> There's one who loves his neighbor as himself;
> And one who cares for naught but fame and self –
> From much corroding care I should be free,
> If once I could determine which is me.

Conscience becomes the courtyard of our decision time for or against Christ. Jammed in our minds are pro-Christ influences, Bible verses, input from Sunday School experience, lingering thoughts from evangelistic services, memories of godly parents or close relatives, fragments from impressive sermons heard or read, the testimony or Christian role models of persons we have met. These voices, however, unless strong at the moment, can be drowned out by those who question, oppose, and scorn Christ. Do not under-estimate the hostile voices against choosing and living for Christ.

> Conscience ... shows with a pointing finger, but no noise,
> A pale procession of past sinful joys,
> All witnesses and blessings foully scorn'd
> Mark these, she says; these, summon'd from afar,
> There find a Judge, inexorably just,
> And perish there as all presumption must.[23]

A mob of secular interests in us demands Jesus' expulsion. A crowd of evil thoughts would shout for Jesus' death, too.

'Away with Him' from our schedules! 'Away with Him' from our thoughts!

Neutral voices are also as dangerous to us as the negative voices. The voice which always calls for postponing a decision for Christ is equally destructive to us.

On judgment day the voices of neutrality and negativism against Christ will be there to shout, as they did before Pilate, for *our* condemnation.

> Sinful thoughts and words unloving,
> Rise against us one by one;
> Acts unworthy, deeds unthinking,
> Good that we have left undone.
> Lord, Thy mercy still entreating,
> We with sin our sins would own;
> From henceforth, the time redeeming,
> May we live to Thee alone.[24]

The Mob in Us

Each person is a walking mob. Each person is occupied by multiple active forces. In terms of our spiritual directions, we ask which crowd we are going to follow.

But God has not left us victims of voices. We have Pilate's problem. That is not in doubt. We know he did not side with Christ. The mob eventually handled him; he did not handle the mob.

If Pilate had only been concerned about spiritual truth, he would have learned from Christ that God is in the crowd control business. When our sins would rise up and holler in hate for our damnation, when the voices of our sins would shout for our destruction, Christ steps in and nullifies their cries.

Past sins cannot divert Christ in His judicial decision to acquit us on the basis of His death for us, and of His imputed righteousness to us. If we are bothered by the voices of sin, which demand our condemnation now, direct the biblical canon on them, one part of which says:

> Therefore there is *now* no condemnation for those who are in Christ Jesus (Rom. 8:1, RSV).

Sins are persistent. They hang on. They come back to pester and create problems. They never tire crying for our destruction. But we must turn over this crowd control problem to Christ. He knows how to handle them.

In July 1603 James I imprisoned Sir Walter Raleigh in the Tower of London on the doubtful charge of treason. He was kept in prison, along with his wife Beth, their two sons (the second son Carew was born in the Tower), and three servants until 1616 (a period of thirteen years). He made good use of his time by reading, praying, writing poems and *A History of the World*. Two years after his release in 1616 he was arrested. He was beheaded at Whitehall, Winchester, in the fall of 1618. Before his execution, he wrote a letter to his wife which contained the following poem.

> From thence to heaven's bribeless hall . . .
> No vain-spent journey;
> For there Christ is the King's attorney,
> Who pleads for all without degrees,
> And He has angels, but no fees.
> When the grand twelve million jury
> Of our sins with direful fury
> 'Gainst our soul black verdicts give,
> Christ pleads His death, and then we live.[25]

APPENDIX ONE:

LEGAL QUESTIONS

In the preceding chapters legal matters have been mentioned because they were integral to Christ's trials. A brief review may be helpful:

1. The ratification meeting of the Sanhedrin, following Christ's appearances before Annas and Caiaphas;
2. Some background on the Great Sanhedrin;
3. Legal obstacles and infractions;
4. The question of the relationship between Roman and Jewish laws.

Undoubtedly, the most influential premise regarding the legal aspects of Christ's trials is theological, rather than juridicial. Yet upon the theological premise rests the starting point of the legal issue. It is the premise that the jurists were pure and committed to fairness. Earlier we raised the issue briefly when we dealt with Christ's appearance before Joseph Caiaphas and the Great Sanhedrin (cf. pp. 45, 46). The premise, ironically, was pivotal in influencing Pilate in his final decision, for he made the same assumption about the crowd as later writers made about the Sanhedrin (pp. 105, 106).

Astonishingly, many are unwilling to grant that corruption had permeated, first, the elite members of Judaism's supreme court, and, second, the general populace. This is a major issue.

The unbiblical concept of innate goodness is reflected, not only in Ellis Rivkin's *What Crucified Jesus?* (referred to on p. 45), but in other works as well. A political journalist, Colin Cross, dismisses the historical credibility of a Sanhedrin trial on the basis that it would have been below them on a holy day. He wrote:

The members of the Sanhedrin were grave men, occupied with the injunctions of the Torah; they would have been concerned with ritual preparations for the great feast rather than with any criminal trial. Would a modern Catholic court be disposed to hear a case on Christmas Day?[1]

Were they so absorbed in their Passover preparations that they had no time for organizing a trial? To say that their court was rigged against Jesus or that He was railroaded to crucifixion some find intolerable.

John Pobee, in his contribution to a collection of essays, *The Trial of Jesus*, said, 'It is difficult to believe that the priests would have sunk to such depths.'[2]

At least three varieties of interpretation have emerged among those who cannot imagine the Sanhedrin to have sought or secured Jesus' death:

1. Those who deny the Jewish court had anything to do with Jesus' trials. Supporters of this view include Hans Lietzmann, Martin Buber, and G. Bornkamm.[3]

2. Some who say a remote section of Jewish justice had anything to do with Jesus' trials. Within this category are those who maintain that Jesus was tried by a political, not the religious Sanhedrin (the two Sanhedrin theory, held by Solomon Zeitlin, and more recently by Ellis Rivkin).[4]

3. Those who say there was only one Sanhedrin, but the Great Sanhedrin in Jerusalem was law-abiding, and had neutral to good intentions. One view says the court had attempted to save Jesus; another that only a barbaric few connived His demise, that only an influential section of the court was involved (Annas, for instance, was behind or at the bottom of Jesus' arrest). Still another view states that there were only brief hearings. The Sanhedrin, in this view, never actually conducted a formal trial. They were law-abiding to the point of handing over to Pilate to carry out a just sentence. Representatives of these variations include Haim

Cohen, Maurice Goquel, R. W. Husband, and J.D.M. Derrett and Eduard Lohse.[5]

View 1 completely jettisons the New Testament as history and reduces the Gospels to early Christian vendetta. This view, in our estimation, lacks sound historical credibility. One need only consult the major histories of the era to see how and where it strays.

View 2 has been recently revived by Ellis Rivkin in his work previously alluded to. In its older form this theory received a devastating debunking by Josef Blinzler in his work. We shall not delve into the particulars of this theory here, except to recommend Blinzler and to note that we hope to present a full examination of Rivkin's arguments in a later publication.

View 3 also reflects the view that the Jewish justices were above a judicial murder. A major contribution to this position was the work of Israeli justice Haim Cohen who interpreted the Sanhedrin role as an attempt to save Jesus. His view was that the Sanhedrin tried to act as a mediator, not prosecutor. Their hope, according to Cohen, was that Jesus be acquitted, but when that failed they tried to have Jesus plead innocent before Pilate.[6]

Another approach was that there was never a full Sanhedrin trial, only a hasty hearing by a few irate members of the court. According to this emphasis it is doubtful that what Jesus went through were trials at all, especially the appearances before Annas and Caiaphas. If they were not trials, then questions of illegality are moot.

However strange this may seem, it has some supporters. But as the following example shows, it tends to exonerate both Jews and Romans alike.

Following Eduard Lohse, J. Duncan M. Derrett in *Law in the New Testament* says that Jesus was brought before an *ad hoc* meeting of a committee within the Sanhedrin. He writes:

> [The Sanhedrin] was obviously primarily a judicial assembly
> convened only for cases of gravity and in an atmosphere of
> deliberation, free from precipitation or haste. Such a court could
> not be swayed easily ... nor [be] readily managed. Jesus was
> not brought before such a body, but before the priestly comm-
> ittee, which exercised the political leadership of the nation.[7]

Of course, on the basis of these views one can completely
evacuate the statements and stories of the Four Gospels. If
one begins with the idea that certain well-educated, religious
leaders had too finely honed moral principles or too dedicated
pious commitments both to law and to custom, then the
accounts in *Matthew*, *Mark*, *Luke*, and *John* are unreliable.

A compromise position, alluded to earlier, straddles the
fence between the historicity of the Gospels and its assumed
special pleading. It is the view that certain priests, who were
not representative of the whole court, were evil. Interwoven
into the fabric of this view is the premise that the religious
leaders were not uniformly and universally opposed to Jesus.
But to treat Jesus' being set up for death as an aberration
does not take seriously the depth of rejection of the Revelation
of God by unsaved persons.

Lawyer-theologian John Warwick Montgomery has
pointed out that it was not far-fetched that Jesus got a raw
deal from representatives of justice, for cases from the period
show Jewish jurists sometimes played fast and loose with
Mishnaic law and procedure.[8] Rabbi Elazar ben Saddok saw
an adulteress executed by fire, whereas the law insisted on
strangulation (*Mishnah*, 'Sanhedrin' 7:2; 11:1). A parallel to
this is found in John 8 where they improvised stoning instead
of the prescribed strangulation (*Mishnah*, tractate 'Ketuboth',
4:3; 'Sanhedrin' 7:9).

For elite religious leaders to stoop to injustice was not an invention of the evangelists, but reflected a reality.[9]

Can the starting point of religious men's goodwill find support in the Four Gospels? Is this starting point in accord with the facts? No, for some very good reasons. If one would isolate Jesus' end from the rest of the Gospels, then the alternative of general goodwill among the justices would seem to have some plausibility. However, these were not detached accounts, but presented as parts of a whole. The witness of the Four Gospels is that there was a hostile atmosphere which arose and grew against Jesus. The opposition to His healings and teachings made the malice of the Sanhedrin a fitting climax to their escalated hatred. And the collusion between a disgruntled disciple of Jesus and His disdainful critics on the court was a 'perfect' match.

Pharisees were friendlier toward Jesus than the more sceptical Sadducees.[10] Pharisee attitudes ranged from curiosity to neutrality. Those who sought private meetings with Him or who didn't mind being seen dining with Him in public, were among those who kept the brakes on a full-scale campaign against Jesus, it would seem. Others were afraid Jesus would set back the relationship with the Romans.

On the other hand, the Gospels show their progressive and pronounced disenchantment with Jesus. They moved from dislike to demonic disgust. Whatever patience there was wore thin; former neutrality turned to rejection.

Rodney A. Whitacre's *Johannine Polemic*, his Cambridge University doctoral dissertation, pointed out that Jesus revealed a startling reality, which the average person, who doesn't make Scripture his guide, finds hard to swallow:

Those who seem to be so virtuous and who are so sure of their favour in the sight of God are found to be farthest from him.... No matter how virtuous the leaders of God's people may appear, nor what they themselves may claim, they are really children of the devil.... This evil which is the source of hatred of the light is the pride and self-satisfaction of the religious people who think they know God and yet are far from him. [11]

The real question, therefore, was not one's standing or status, but the response to revelation. The 'final solution to the Jesus problem' was the negative reaction to Him as divine revelation. The clearer the revelation, the sharper the rejection. The trial sequence fits into a pattern. The Gospel of John, in particular, shows how unbelief showed its head from the very inception of the revelation. The unique feature of John is that it depicts faith and doubt arising from the same circumstances and concepts, and how they grew and became more intense. (Other Gospels, such as Mark, beginning in chapter 3, show a rejection syndrome but not with the same degree or depth.)

Consider John chapter 5, where there was a hostile reaction as a result of the healing of the man who was lame for thirty-eight years. The reader is prepared by the evangelist for what was behind Jesus' trouble with the authorities in the earlier statement: 'Everyone who does evil hates the light, and will not come into the light' (3:20). In chapter 5, opposition to Him was openly expressed among the hierarchy (5:16).

When the light of revelation falls upon them, they themselves are unmasked for what they are, and not just their works. Thus their 'hatred' has a psychological explanation and is also rooted in a profounder level of their being; it comes from a general attitude for which they are responsible and which is totally corrupt. This is why they do not 'come to the light'.... In the same way, in [John] 5:40-47, Jesus throws light on the hidden depths of the heart and unmasks the unbelieving Jews as men who do not seek God but their own vainglory, so estranged from God by nature that they cannot believe God's envoy.[12]

The position of the New Testament is unanimous on the matter of the average man's aversion to the rule of God.

Indeed, the more religious a person is and the more respected by his peers, the greater difficulty that person finds in abandoning his own righteousness to rely solely upon the righteousness of Christ. This is one of two crucial issues.

Does the amount of space devoted to this matter belong in a section dealing with the legal questions? It is important because it provides the basis for the misuse, avoidance, and use of law for the goal of silencing Jesus.

Other major questions are historical, rather than theological. They have to do with whether the codified Jewish law, *The Mishnah*, which has been cited at various places in the preceding sections, reflected Sanhedrin law practice in the time of Jesus. It is this matter we must address next.

While the Roman law was the best developed and already past its classical period, Jewish law was not codified.[13] In New Testament times the Jewish law was still in its oral form.[14] The *Mishnah*, which I have cited at various points, was a late second century compilation of oral tradition by Rabbi Judah ha-Nasi.[15] Yet it did reflect the oral tradition current in Pharisaism when Jesus lived.[16]

The *Mishnah* represented both Pharisaic idealization and toleration. Their rules were more humane than harsh. The fact that not a single Pharisaic rule was followed in Jesus' trial before Caiaphas proved, to Blinzler, that only Sadducean rules were observed (cf. Blinzler's 1961 article, 'Das Syndedrium von Jerusalem und die Strafprozessordnung der Mischna,' *Zeitschrift für die neutestamentliche Wissenschaft*, LII, 60). This view fits with the recognized fact that the Sadducees controlled the Great Sanhedrin in Jesus' time. His conclusion was that 'tractate "Sanhedrin" [which] did not yet apply in Jewish penal law in the period before AD 70 ... can be regarded as unshaken'.[17] And the Sadducean rules were typically severe.[18]

Because the *Mishnah* came after the period of Christ's life, does that constitute sufficient ground for dismissing tractate 'Sanhedrin' as a legal guideline in determining whether or not and to what extent Jesus was the victim of injustices? J. Duncan M. Derrett, for example, dismissed the attempt of F. J. Powell to show how the *Mishnah* was violated in the Jewish trials, saying 'the banal outcome of such an investigation never struck the author as incongruous'.[19] According to Derrett's opinion:

> Attempts to read the puzzling accounts of the trial of Jesus in the light of Mishnaic law are very common, but often futile.[20]

W. R. Wilson, in a more recent work, was of the same opinion, i.e. that the *Mishnah* material has little bearing 'because their date and authenticity are uncertain'.[21]

Derrett, we have seen, considered the approach of Powell incongruous in view of the *Mishnah* being a second century work. But Derrett's conclusion was worse than banal and incongruous. He held 'Jesus' death was nobody's fault'.[22] He argued that the trials were bound to happen and were meant to happen – that the trials were moral!

Josef Blinzler, along with M. Jean Imbert, Professor in the Faculty of Law and Economics at Paris, however, has advocated the reliableness of the New Testament records on the trials of Christ. In his work on the Trials of Christ Blinzler has an Excursus entitled, 'On the Question of whether the Mishnaic Criminal Code was in Operation at the time of Jesus', in which he examines the pros and cons concerning to what degree any of the written laws could reflect unwritten, practiced law of Jesus' era. His treatment merits careful reading.

Blinzler cites Abrahams, a foremost Talmudic scholar, who maintained that several historical details in the Gospels intimate that what came later in the Mishnah were not necessarily expunged rules or not yet in effect when Christ lived.[23] The overlapping portions of old and new laws come to a minimum of five, the first two of which were pointed out by Abrahams and the latter three I have added:

1. The tearing of the high priest's garment (Matt. 26:65; *Sanhedrin* 7:5B)

2. The offering of a narcotic drink to those about to be crucified (Matt. 27:34; *T. B. Sanhedrin* in 43a)

3. The practice of stoning (one of the four forms of capital punishment) prescribed in the *Mishnah* (*Sanhedrin* 7.10), attempted several times on Jesus (John 8:59; 10:31).

4. The practice of no man being condemned unheard (John 7:51) confirmed by a Rabbinic source.

5. Forbidding of the admission of evidence by a single witness (John 8:17), which was a carry-over from the Old Testament, also has support from the same Rabbinic sources.[24]

When Jesus was tried the *Mishnah* was not in force in the exact form of the tractates; yet if Jewish tradition followed form, they really were in effect even though lacking word-for-word conformity.[25]

Blinzler's conclusion (without argumentation) follows:

Everything that has hitherto been attacked as an illegality in the trial of Jesus, in view of the criminal code outlined in the Mishna [sic], was completely in accordance with the criminal code then in force, which was a Sadducean code, and did not know or recognize those pharisaic, humanitarian features of the Mishna code which were not founded on the Old Testament.[26]

123

The *Mishnah* today (the Danby edition is the standard and still in print) must be used with caution, for it reflects Pharisaic rules, not Sadducean rules. It is widely recognized that the Great Sanhedrin was dominated by the Sadducees, not the Pharisees.[27]

From start to finish Jesus' trials broke Jewish and Roman Law. Despite the disregard Derrett and others have expressed toward this facet, there is value in outlining the violations.

Before that, it should be noted that Jesus was deliberately and sequentially deprived of justice. Isaiah 53:8 in the Septuagint reads 'in his humiliation his judgment was taken away,' in the sense of 'withheld'. This was cited in Acts 8:33 (NEB): 'He has been humiliated and has no redress.' Philip, the Evangelist, presented this as being fulfilled in Jesus. It is still regarded as one of the greatest Messianic passages in the Old Testament.

Even if one takes the position that the *Mishnah* guidelines reflected much of what was or could have been followed in Jesus' trials, this does not produce unanimity on the matter of how many breaches there were. While Blinzler, for instance, could not agree on the exact number of violations,[28] nevertheless, he held strongly to the position that the Sanhedrin was guilty of 'very serious infringement of the Law.'[29]

Tabulations vary as to how many laws were broken. Some say twenty-seven;[30] others say less.

'At what juncture does one begin to look for violations of law?' If one does not confine oneself to the trials, but includes the arrest, then the number of illegalities will grow. If one were to consider Jesus' own listing of injustices (which is not inconceivable), then it would seem that the arrest should be included, for on the night of actual arrest He protested that they came after Him as if He were a guerilla bandit (Mark 14:48).[31] Also, the variance in counting illegalities will depend on the particular commentators, but their inability to agree on each instance does not annul the conviction that Jesus suffered injustice and that His trials were a mockery of judicial order, Jewish and Roman.

Therefore, there is some warrant in drawing up a list of illegalities, however imprecise or incomplete they may be. The only standard for Jewish Law is based on the tractate 'Sanhedrin', *The Mishnah* translated and edited by Herbert Danby [New York: Oxford University Press, 1933]. Under three judges there were no less than twenty-one violations of law, Jewish and Roman:

Under Annas

1. The arrest was not justifiable since Jesus was not charged with a capital offence.

2. A night arrest was illegal.

3. The arresting party was mainly Temple police known as 'Shoterim.' (Num. 8:24, 25; Deut. 20: 5-9; Luke 22:52.) John alone mentions the presence of Roman soldiers (18:12). The number of Roman soldiers may have been large, because a 'chiliarch' (equivalent to our army colonel) was present and a chiliarch was in charge of 1,000 soldiers. Yet the charge against Jesus, at first, was not political. It was improper for Rome to be present. (This was a strong indication of collusion between Annas/Caiaphas and Pilate).

4. Judas' deposition was invalid, for according to Leviticus 19:16-18, the testimony of an accomplice was illegal.

5. The hit on the head during the hearing was unwarranted and unfair, a travesty of justice.

125

6. Annas had no legal right to act as Judge, since his term as President of the Great Sanhedrin ceased AD 14.

Under Joseph Caiaphas

7. Capital cases could not be tried at night (*Sanhedrin* 4:1).

8. Capital judgments were to be delayed to the next day (*Sanhedrin* 4:1). The death sentence could not be given on the same day of the trial.

9. Capital cases could not be tried on the eve of a Sabbath or of a festival day such as Passover (*Sanhedrin* 4:1).

10. It was illegal to pass the death sentence except in the Hall of Hewn Stone, which was next to the Temple.

11. An attempt was to be made to find witnesses *for* the defence (*Sanhedrin* 5:4). The Sanhedrin considered themselves absolved from considering the other side. Evidence for the defendant Jesus was suppressed and denied.

12. In conjunction with this, capital cases were to open with arguments for acquittal (*Sanhedrin* 4:1).

13. False witnesses were sought – but any false witness was to suffer condign penalties (*Sanhedrin* 11:6).

14. Younger members of the court were to speak first so as not to be influenced by the older members (*Sanhedrin* 4:2). Caiaphas, however, dominated the proceedings, according to the Gospels. He was more eager to conclude the session and condemn Jesus than he was to

elicit the truth. He prejudiced the court, also, apparently cutting off debate. Moreover, representatives of the Jewish court, when Jesus was before Pilate, did their best to play upon the prejudices of the crowd.

15. In capital cases all could not speak in favour of condemnation (*Sanhedrin* 4:1), but Caiaphas clearly solicited this unanimity.

16. It was illegal to question the defendant unless the witnesses agreed. If the prosecution failed to make out a *prima facie* case, there was no right to question the accused. 'The judge was not entitled to make up for the shortcomings of the prosecution by questioning the accused.'[32] Caiaphas was overly eager to circumvent legal guidelines in order to expedite his decision to have Jesus destroyed. Caiaphas used insinuation, lies, badgering, self-incrimination of the defendant (confession), and abjuration under oath to implement his previously made-up intent.

17. A person could only be condemned by the minimum of two witnesses, not by his own confession. Without agreeing witnesses there was no case and should be no trial. The witnesses constituted the charge. Witnesses were prosecutors (*Sanhedrin* 6:1, 2, 3, 4 with Deut. 17:7).[33]

18. The mockery by the court (Matt. 26:67, 68) was out of place and showed a complete disregard for law and order.

Under Pilate

19. Pilate's refusal to rubber-stamp the findings of the Great Sanhedrin showed signs of commitment to justice, but as the trials continued, it became clear that Pilate was victimized by his fears, by his disdain, and by his ambitions. In the end he gave in to popular demand.

20. Pilate's supposition that Jesus belonged to Antipas' jurisdiction because He lived there was wrong, as well as his thinking that Jesus' referral to Herod would get rid of the case. Pilate found no grounds of insurrection or sedition in Jesus. Indeed, three times he declared Jesus innocent of the charges (Luke 23:4, 14, 22). If Pilate really believed Jesus was innocent, the case was finished and He should have been dismissed or freed. Even then it was wrong to try a man twice. Therefore, it was illegal to send Him on to Herod Antipas. Antipas' return of Jesus, on the other hand, re-established Jesus' innocence!

21. The scourging without a formal sentence was illegal. Pilate never pronounced a formal sentence, it seems, perhaps thinking that the tablet inscription was enough. Blinzler, however, thought Mark 15:15 meant a formal death sentence was issued.[34] The title over the cross may have been his last attempt to giving the semblance of legality to a trial over which he had lost control. Pilate did not succeed in thwarting the wishes of Jesus' enemies, but gave in to their threats, thereby abandoning justice.

The Question of the Relationship of Jewish and Roman Law

All evidence points to the reliability of the notation in John 18:31 that Rome alone had the right to capital punishment.[35] Forty years before the destruction of Jerusalem the Sanhedrin's right to take a life was taken away.[36] This was also confirmed in the *Talmud*.[37]

In *Figure 1*, is a visualized picture of the inter-relationship of Roman and Jewish law. Only one exception is known. There existed on the books a restricted right for the Great Sanhedrin to utilize capital punishment. But such was never

Figure 1

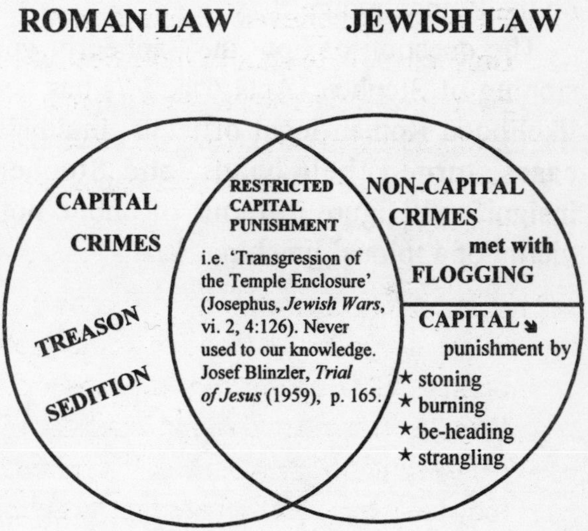

ROMAN LAW   JEWISH LAW

CAPITAL CRIMES

TREASON

SEDITION

RESTRICTED CAPITAL PUNISHMENT
i.e. 'Transgression of the Temple Enclosure' (Josephus, *Jewish Wars*, vi. 2, 4:126). Never used to our knowledge. Josef Blinzler, *Trial of Jesus* (1959), p. 165.

NON-CAPITAL CRIMES met with FLOGGING

CAPITAL punishment by
★ stoning
★ burning
★ be-heading
★ strangling

used.[38] Evidence exists that Roman practice tried to honour Jewish custom, such as in the scruple of taking down bodies in honour of the Sabbath (John 19:31). But on the death penalty Rome had absolute authority. The fact of an actual Sanhedrin trial is established by Matthew 27:3, for the condemnation Judas learned of was the condemnation by the

Jewish court.[39] Mark reports a Sanhedrin death sentence.

The question immediately comes to mind: 'Why would the Sanhedrin conduct a trial of Jesus if they knew beforehand that they could not put Jesus to death?' They felt a compulsion to go through the form of a trial in order to appear legal. As James Moffatt wrote:

> They were kept within judicial limits only so far as it was necessary to save appearances.[40]

This was an important value, as they saw it. Through their trial and conclusion they could go to Pilate with an official verdict (yet not telling him for which one they initially condemned Jesus). 'It was a means of exerting moral pressure on the Roman judge.'[41]

The question of how the Sanhedrin got away with the stoning of Stephen (Acts 6 and 7) has been raised. In all likelihood Roman legal officials, in smaller, less volatile cases, turned their heads, and Stephen, who was an insignificant figure in terms of public notice, became the victim of a 'pious' lynching.[42]

APPENDIX TWO:

ONE OR TWO TEMPLE CLEANSINGS?

At several points in the main body of the present study I maintained that Christ cleansed the Temple in the first week of His ministry (John 2:12-22) and once again at the conclusion of His ministry, during His last week (Matt. 21:12-17; Mark 11:12-19; Luke 19:45-48).

Strong textual arguments support two cleansings. Before we look at those, the rationale of those who think there was only one Temple cleansing should be examined. Most grant that Jesus cleansed the Temple just after the Palm Sunday parade. Typical film versions of Christ's life acknowledge a last week, not a first week, cleansing of the Temple. Alan H. McNeile represented those who hold to one Temple cleansing. He wrote 'that the event happened twice is hardly conceivable'.[1]

J. H. Bernard, another respected commentator, wrote:

> On psychological grounds, the incident [in John] is hardly credible, if it is to be put at the beginning of the ministry of Jesus.[2]

Was the placement of the Temple cleansing in John correct? Had he confused it with a later cleansing? That would mean he restructured the traditional chronology of Jesus' ministry.

Some have argued that the atmosphere of the first week did not warrant a cleansing then. E. F. Scott, and others, have argued that during the first week of Jesus' ministry there just was not a confrontational, cathartic mood to warrant the cleansing as there was in the last week.[3]

Admittedly, it took some time for opposition against Jesus to come to a head. Those unsympathetic to Jesus' deity claims say His massive assault on the Temple was because His followers had provided the necessary emotional support He needed for that venture. It was obviously true that after three years His twelve workers were in a better position to understand what He was about. Although towards the end Jesus' closest followers crumbled, prior to the final assault on Jesus, it must be said that He had greater support at the end of His ministry than at the start. It is questionable, however, that His disciples were a support group. Did Jesus think He needed their participation to chase out the sheep/dove booth operators?

John's account of the Temple cleansing showed Jesus' act of cleansing was solitary and considered counter-productive to an extended ministry, even suicidal (John 2:17).

A late symbolic cleansing had much more drama and was more fitting because Judaism's leadership penchant for retaliation against Jesus had grown. In none of the Gospels is the Temple cleansing presented as a desperate act of a frustrated reformer. The second cleansing of the Temple showed greater intensity, for Jesus' exodus was fast approaching. A delayed second cleansing showed some exasperation, for after all, Jesus maintained a lofty vision for the Temple.

Would the cleansing reflect poorly on Jesus' style, ambition and character? In neither cleansing was Jesus simply reacting. He was acting. The early Temple cleansing acknowledged – in so many words – a depth of clerical and institutional corruption. Jesus' anger against Gentiles being forcibly blocked from a place of worship by the occupancy of the Court of the Gentiles was, we contend, evident both at the start and conclusion of His earthly ministry.

Arguments for maintaining two cleansings are as follows:

1. John had access to and reflected awareness of the other accounts. He has provided historical details of Christ's life not mentioned in the Synoptics – the first Temple cleansing is such a detail. Unless the Temple cleansings

chronology is kept, all other chronological notations in John are to be questioned. If the placement of the cleansing was mistakenly put early, then all Johannine chronological distinctives are unreliable and irrelevant.

2. There are significant differences between the two cleansings, which warrant keeping them separate:
   a. The statement about destroying and raising up is not found in the Synoptics.
   b. The first cleansing did not stop the abuses, but Jesus did not lower His ideal to fit the entrenched Temple misuse.

   A second cleansing emphasized His fearlessness and His implacable disdain for the abuse of the Temple without a let-up or slackening. To maintain both cleansings gives support to those who see Jesus' perceptive powers as sharp at the start as at the finish. He would not condone at the end of His ministry what he opposed at the start.

3. Surely, if one grants several raisings from the dead, repeated sermons and parables, repeated feedings, etc., there should be no problem in accepting two cleansings. The repetition of a prophetic act was appropriate, for it indicated that there was early opposition to Jesus.

4. An early cleansing provides a partial fulfilment of what John the Baptist said at Jesus' baptism – that he would purge with fire (Matt. 3:11; cf. Mal. 3:2-4). Although no actual fire was used in the Temple cleansings, there was a holy fire in Jesus which consumed His desires.

5. A single late Temple cleansing would not fit Psalm 69:9 which is cited in John 2:17 by His disciples. By the time of the last week His disciples had been told many times

that His arrest was imminent. Psalm 69:9 best belongs to an early cleansing. Leon Morris has noted, 'Despite the assertions of some ... there are practically no resemblances between the narratives, apart from the central act.'[4]

6. A positive response to Jesus in Jerusalem was never there from the start. John makes that certain. Early opposition to Jesus' healings was clear in Mark (3:6). A negative atmosphere was in the first week also.

7. John's attention to physical detail in his Gospel (stone jars, not clay – 2:6; actual count of crowd – 6:10-13; number of fish caught – 21:11) along with his scrupulous sense of time and place (cf. 3:24; 4:6) would mean that the first Temple cleansing was where the Gospel has it, without denying the second cleansing which he doesn't mention.

Raymond E. Brown recognized the latter argument and suggested a compromise position – i.e. that the veiled statement about His death and resurrection had been given early in Jesus' ministry, and inserted in the story of the Temple cleansing in His last week.[5] But this idea lacks force, for John 2:19-21 cannot be separated from John 2:17 and 2:22, the verses which immediately precede and follow the passage, verses Brown wishes to confine to the early ministry of Jesus. Both 2:17 and 2:22 belong with 2:19-21 together; they are a unit. Yet in the case of 2:17 an immediate physical repercussion is feared to come against Jesus for His action and in 2:22 a time lapse is necessary for the verse to have any historical credibility. Both verses speak strongly that the entire series of sayings belong exclusively to a first cleansing.

Two cleansings have a lot going for them.[6] They fit together chronologically, textually, and theologically:

Chronologically

An early assault on Temple commercialism and High Priestly greed helps explain why Jesus had to flee Judea and seek relative safety in the north, in Galilee (John 4:1-3). R. V. G. Tasker wrote:

> It was because Jesus made his early attack upon traditional Pharisaic worship at the capital, that the mission of scribes was sent from Jerusalem to Galilee, when they entered upon what was virtually a 'counter-attack' by the assertion that Jesus was possessed by Beelzebub. This mission is mentioned without any explanation of its origin, in Mark 3:22.[7]

Textually

C. H. Dodd has effectively argued for the independence of John's history.[8] John gives a description of the Temple cleansing which is uniquely different from the others. These differences include: the matter of the merciful treatment of the pigeon owners/sellers (2:16) and the advancement of His awareness of the corruption (from the Johannine phrase 'house of merchandise' [John 2:16] to 'den of marauders' (Mark 11:17]).

Theologically

Early rejection of Jesus by the religious rulers followed in line with the critical calling-on-the-carpet of John the Baptist who dared suggest that card-carrying Jews needed to be washed from their sins and to testify to that in public baptism (John 1:19-25). The fact that Jesus dared to cleanse the Temple at the start of His ministry explains why there was a consistent opposition to Him by the religious hierarchs.

Jesus' first cleansing of the Temple did not stimulate reform. There was no attempt nor aim on the part of Annas and Caiaphas to change and clear out the animals-for-sale from the Court of the Gentiles. Indeed, the reaction was to dig in and maintain this practice. The Sadducees

> went to great length to protect their power and prestige; many
> of their ceremonial positions, [P. Z.] Lauterbach observes,
> benefited the priests financially.[9]

This went to show that the corruption fostered and furthered by Annas and Caiaphas, who were the principal benefactors of the operation, was irradicable and inveterate. Profiteering by the priests made Jesus' blood boil. Operating under the guise of devotion to God and ministering to the needs of the people, a great offence to the Lord was being perpetuated. The double cleansing reinforced the early disclosure – that the dry rot of secularism and the poisoned air of personal greed had taken captive the top officials of the nation.

The two assaults of Jesus on their personal money-making schemes explain why they were driven nearly mad with the desire, swiftly and finally, to do away with Jesus.

Their fury over Jesus' forays into the Temple provides the emotional explanation of why He was arrested, framed, and executed. Revenge for exposing their vice would not be tolerated or forgiven. Jesus was to pay for His intrusions and the 'rude' interruptions of their enterprise. He had made a small dent on their profits at two Passovers, but He made an even 'worse' mark in exposing their image among the people. Hell has no fury like churchmen out to retaliate.

APPENDIX THREE:

ACADEMIC SMOKE and MIRRORS?

Much of modern scholarship pooh-poohs conservative conclusions on the passion records. Several instances are cited in the preceding chapters. Many readers will not have access to or buy monographs on the trials of Christ, nor will they wade through tomes on the subject. But they may visit libraries and turn to encyclopedia articles. I wish to point out two recent articles in an academically rich Bible dictionary set which stand in sharp contrast to what I have found and have written. Below I've culled the salient points from the two articles. After reading my extractions, make a comparison with what I have supplied earlier in the body of the chapters dealing with Annas and Caiaphas, then decide which better conforms to the historic gospel materials.

Does the Gospel of John, for instance, unjustly blame Annas and Caiaphas with criminality in their roles in the arrest and trial of Jesus? Bruce Chilton, now on the faculty of Bard College, on the other hand, writing on Annas and Caiaphas in *The Anchor Bible Dictionary* is a recent representative of those who say the trial narratives in the gospels did not implicate Annas and Caiaphas as key fomenters in Jesus' arrest and Sanhedrin condemnation.[1]

Take Annas. Chilton bends over backwards in putting an innocent construction on Annas' role in the animal sales in the Temple grounds. To attribute greed, vindictiveness, and deep hate in Annas against Jesus for disrupting the money-making project is – according to Chilton – to 'indulge the rhetorical reference to Annas in the NT than to describe it.' Again, 'to speculate on [Annas'] character – and especially to suggest that his motivation was economic – is to proceed far beyond the evidence and to desert exegesis in favor of a long-discredited, apologetic stance.'

Chilton's near-eager bent on trying to exonerate Joseph Caiaphas also comes across when he writes: 'Caiaphas is emblematic of the opposition without being an instigator of it.' More astonishing, Chilton wrote: 'Caiaphas emerges most clearly as a personality in John, in close association with Jesus' passion, but he does not emerge as an active or willing agent of Jesus' execution ... [on the basis of Caiaphas' early comment that it is expedient that one die for the people (11:47-53) Chilton continues] no malice is ascribed to Caiaphas.' At that point, perhaps, Chilton's overall implication neglected to mention the chief priest's scathing interrogation and denunciation of Jesus with abuse. Jesus was not guilty of blasphemy, but Caiaphas was. All the indicators point to a personal well of ire and a bottomless pit of revenge that funneled and fueled along through the night. The Sanhedrin plot was to corral and squash Jesus' program; it had a retaliatory inclination. The bent and bias of the Sanhedrin was building for three years.

Chilton is unrealistic to suggest that up to John 18:15-24 Caiaphas was 'a bystander to the action'. In a similar vein, Chilton says, '[Caiaphas] is more moved by events than he influences them.' The Johannine material, Chilton would attempt to establish, truncates Caiaphas' role in Jesus' sentence of death and 'denies him any dramatic place in the action'. The claims become increasingly outrageous and ridiculous when Chilton writes: 'No judgment of Caiaphas' character or motivation can make any serious claim on our attention, except as an imaginative exercise. Historically speaking, the available evidence will not permit conclusions of that sort.'

The accounts of the Gospels are almost said to be sympathetic to Annas and Caiaphas if we are to believe Chilton. Chilton's depiction of Annas and his son-in-law's intentions mutes and muffles their evil intentions. To underplay the evil in Annas and Caiaphas is to have us read the Gospels with blinders. I contend that Chilton fogs the trail of conniving, calculating religious felons.

What he wrote comes close to an academic white wash! The Gospels transparently implicate Caiaphas in Jesus' condemnation. Mark 3:6 and John 5:18 indicate that Jesus' death was plotted early on (the Passover plot was against him, not by Him). This was seen by the evangelist John (7:1), by the people of Jerusalem (Jn. 7:25), and by Jesus Himself (7:19; 8:37). Numerous times the Gospels fingered (in the sense of identified, not that the evangelists maligned them) the 'chief priests'. Josef Blinzler wrote: 'Mistrust turned to open enmity and enmity hardened to moral hatred.... The mortal enmity which the ruling circles cherished toward Jesus had personal, political, nationalistic and religious grounds'.[2] In Acts, Peter summarized and repeated what is stuck fast in history, that Caiaphas conspired, plotted, sought, expedited, and effected our Lord's being brought before Roman justice for crucifixion.

Should one argue for Annas' and Caiaphas' hesitant involvement, fringe guilt, or even innocence? The Gospel records intimate that a chief grudge was kept alive by the chief priests. Chilton has been given grounds in the narratives themselves warranting more than his concession that Caiaphas 'did engineer the installation of vendors in the temple'. Christians down the centuries have accurately described Annas and Caiaphas ruthless, not righteous, not respectable.

Is that assessment severe and undeserving? Have I unfairly vilified those two leaders? The villainy worth lamenting is the villainy that mishandled and unjustly tried and condemned the holy Son of God. Could anything be more severe than engineering Jesus' death? Rather than being noble leaders, under the surface they were nefarious rogues, ripe with reprisal. Both Annas and Caiaphas were demonically devious, in the grips of and guided by moral turpitude. They had proper pedigree, but because of their active role from the beginning they were led along by the evil of their natures.

   Bear in mind that the New Testament emphasizes that it
was not just isolated individuals who rejected Christ, but the
nation of Israel, through their representatives and finally
through their own voice and vote, sought Jesus' execution
and elimination (John 1:11). The chief priests played a
substantial role in railroading Jesus, but in the shouts of the
ordinary citizenry for Jesus' crucifixion Israel proved to be
unified in their desire. Thus, it became 'the action of the
nation, and this understanding of events controls the entire
Gospel record.'[3]

APPENDIX FOUR:

SO-CALLED ANTI-JEWISHNESS
IN THE GOSPELS

The present work on Christ's trials represents the view point that some first-century Jewish elite played a significant role in Jesus' arrest, trial, and death. (See earlier comments in the Introduction, pages 21, 22, especially note # 27). I have not raised an esoteric minuscule historical aside, for the subject is not one that occurs just to scholars or to those in academia. Careful and attentive readers of the primary documents of Christianity meet it on their own.

Without being prodded by modern research, the ordinary Bible reader wonders about the accuracy of Jewish complicity in Jesus' death. Fortunately, some valuable monographs dealing with Christ's Passion, trials, and death have appeared in the last decade of the 20th century. The purpose of this Appendix is to alert the modern reader of several recent studies that bear significantly on the subject, and provide challenges.

An Exegetical Mine

One indispensable tool in re-examining the Gospel Passion narratives is Raymond Brown's highly praised, seminal work, *The Death of the Messiah* (1994). The trials material, which I have briefly covered in the preceding commentary, occupy a whopping 470 pages in Brown's Volume One.

Brown offered his opinions on both the role of the Jewish authorities and on the question of the responsibility for the death of Jesus in Volume 1: 382-397. For those who don't have immediate access to the work, I supply some selections:

"All the Gospels agree that the Jewish authorities, particularly the priests, disliked Jesus and that there were earlier attempts to stop his teaching. All agree on a judicial action by the Sanhedrin, [footnote # 128] and (if we join Acts to Luke) all agree that one of the issues against Jesus was the threatened destruction of the Temple sanctuary. All agree that the Jewish authorities gave Jesus over to Pilate, who sentenced him to death.... If one takes the

Gospels at face value (and even if one examines them through the microscope of historical criticism), there emerges a Jesus capable of generating intense dislike.[148] Indeed, that is the usual result of asking self-consciously religious people to change their minds (which is what is meant literally by metanoia)....The Gospel portrait implies that Jesus would be found guilty by the self-conscious religious majority of any age and background."

Three other up-to-date and thorough examinations, not previously cited, also warrant mention. Don't overlook an anthology published in 1993. More likely to escape notice is a doctoral dissertation published in 1994. Lastly, those outside the United States will have missed another book by a Catholic publishing house, which should be cited.

An Anthology

Craig A. Evans and Donald A. Hagner, co-edited *Anti-Semitism and Early Christianity* (Issues of Polemic and Faith), with a Foreward by James A. Sanders [Minneapolis: Fortress Press, 1993], a collection of essays by 13 specialists. It covers three areas: Section I: Antecedents of New Testament Polemic; Section II: Anti-Semitism and the New Testament Writings; and Section III: Anti-Semitism and Post-New Testament Writings.

For our purposes the most immediate application to the subject of the trials of Christ is Section II. Four out of the eight essays in Section II (pp. 55- 214) bear directly on the Gospels: "A Loyal Critic: Matthew's Polemic with Judaism in Theological Perspective" by Scot McKnight; "Anti-Semitism and/or Anti-Judaism in Mark?" by Robert A. Guelich; "'Fighting against God': Luke's Interpretation of Jewish Rejection of the Messiah Jesus" by David L. Tiede; "Anti-Semitism and the Gospel of John" by Robert Kysar.

Limitations of space prevent both a substantial critique and extensive summary of these useful articles. Readers are encouraged to check them out for their detailed argumentation. All of them bear especially on Jesus' trials, and whether or not the Synoptic Gospels and John are intrinsically or intentionally anti-Jewish.

MATTHEW: McKnight's conclusion: "Matthew's Gospel, however harsh and unpleasant to modern sensitivities, is not anti-Semitic. It is, on the contrary, a compassionate but vigorous appeal to nonmessianic Judaism to respond to the Messiah.....Matthew does not hesitate to use the harsh rhetoric of condemnation for those who opt to reject Jesus. But Matthew's rhetoric is conventional, unabrasive for his time, and founded upon his theological convictions (salvation-historical and christological.)"

MARK: Guelich's summary: "The scribes...in Mark's story share much of the Pharisees' concern about Jesus' regard for the Law, do participate actively along with the chief priests in arranging for his death. These two groups first come together to plot Jesus' death when he declares judgment on the Temple (11:18). They work together as members of the Sanhedrin to condemn Jesus (14:53-65), and they stand together at the crucifixion to mock the 'Messiah, King of Israel' (15:31-32). Yet it is the chief priests who carry the final responsibility for Jesus' death by accusing Jesus before Pilate and inciting the crowd to persuade Pilate to release Barabbas rather than Jesus (15:2-11)." Guelich's conclusion: "...a careful, historical, literary reading of Mark's narrative will demonstrate that one can in no way speak of 'anti-Semitism' and only in a highly qualified manner of 'anti-Judaism' in Mark's Gospel."

LUKE: Like most scholars David Tiede deals not with the Gospel of Luke alone, but with Luke-Acts, since Luke authored both the Gospel and the Acts, and both books deal with the elements of causation of Jesus' crucifixion. One should look at Tiede's full analysis, of course, but he says "in [the] spectrum of Judaean conflict, Luke's narrative is neither more nor less anti-Jewish than the other sources." The variety of repentant Jews in Luke-Acts has the effect of softening an unrelenting anti-Jewish tone. (In the book below Weatherly has 2 pages on Tiede.)

JOHN: Robert Kysar notes, as others, that the negative reactions to Jesus conveyed in the phrase "the Jews" should be balanced with the instances where there were neutral inquiries, surprising sympathetic responses to Jesus, even places where Jesus saw himself Jewish or praises Judaism. Sometimes not every participant in the events, though patently Jewish, are linked with "the [pejorative] Jews." In one instance the Pharisees who opposed Jesus were not to be lumped with the authorities who believed (12:42). But Jesus Himself is said to identify official Judaism with the spirit of the world and the realm of unbelief. Kysar says this results in John having an anti-Jewish flavor. Most disappointing is Kysar's willingness to doubt whether such a Gospel should have been considered authentic canon. Readers, faced with the argument of John and the reported stance of Jesus, must decide whether or not humans retain and exercise an instinctive revulsion for divine light. Also requiring our decision is the truth of the hope-giving proposition in the preface that only divine light can overcome particular spiritual darkness, a seemingly minor proposition that supports the Gospel of John's clear arguments elsewhere for divine predestination.

A 1991 Aberdeen Scotland doctoral dissertation on the Luke-Acts area by Jon A. Weatherly, New Testament professor at Cincinnati Bible Seminary, deserves reference (Jon A. Weatherly, *Jewish Responsibility for the Death of Jesus in Luke-Acts* [Sheffield, UK: Sheffield Academic Press, 1994], Journal for the Study of the New Testament, Supplement Series 106, 307 pages.)

DISSERTATION ON ALLEGED ANTI-SEMITISM IN LUKE-ACTS

To my knowledge Weatherly's book is probably the most thorough, recent study about the supposed anti-Jewishness of the Luke-Acts writings. Conducted under the supervision of Dr. Howard Marshall, the monograph deals with the following subsections:

Chapter 1—A Review of Research on Judaism and the Death of Jesus in Luke-Acts;

Chapter 2—Jerusalem's Responsibility for the Death of Jesus in Luke-Acts;

Chapter 3—Jerusalem's Responsibility in relation to all Israel;

Chapter 4—Responsibility for the Death of Jesus in Paul: 1 Thessalonians 2:14-16;

Chapter 5—Responsibility for the Death of Jesus in Pre-Synoptic Tradition;

Chapter 6—Origins of Jerusalem's Responsibility for the Death of Jesus in Acts;

Chapter 7—Transmission of Traditions of Responsibility for the Death of Jesus;

Chapter 8—Conclusions

Chapter 1 provides vital background to the subject. In it he reviews the contributions of the 22 scholars on the subject: Pre-W.W.II (Classical Modern Scholarship): Ferdinand Christian Baur; Franz Overbeck; Alfred Loisy; Adolf Harnack; Martin Dibelius. Post-W.W.II (Modern Scholarship):Hans Conzelmann; Ernst Haenchen; Joachim Gnilka; John C. O'Neill; Ulrich Wilckens; Robert Maddox; Stephen G. Wilson; Joseph B. Tyson; Jack T. Sanders. Dissent from the Consensus: Gerhard Lohfink; Eric Franklin; Jacques Dupont; Augustin George; Jacob Jervell; David L. Tiede; Robert L. Brawley; David P. Moessner.

Central to Weatherly's thesis is his examination of key

passages. (John's Gospel was not part of his examination.) Especially important are those pivotal Lukan passages sometimes used to exonerate clerical Judaism from responsibility for Jesus' arrest and crucifixion. Weatherly shows the flaws in certain writers and provides the Scriptural interpretations which fit the contexts and corroborative information. Of particular interest for students of Jesus' trials is Weatherly's coverage of the role of the high priests (pp. 198-210). They both plotted Jesus' arrest, instigated His condemnation, and insured Jesus' death. They were Jesus' leading opponents who solicited and gained the co-operation of significant associate Pharisees. By the same token, the gullible Jewish public aligned themselves with the rulers in their assessments and wishes.

Weatherly's conclusions are that the Lukan evidence supports the position that key Jewish Jerusalem officials and the people of Jerusalem were responsible for Jesus' crucifixion, without any attempt to ameliorate Gentile responsibility. Neither in Luke nor in Acts did the writer try to denigrate Jews generally. The other Gospels and John, and the background material from St. Paul, support the same position, which is consistent with the empirical historical data.

Israel was divided on how to react to Jesus. There was no monolithic response to Jesus in Judaism. Some accepted, but many rejected. Because of those instances of Jewish alignment with Jesus, a mission to unbelieving Israel never ceased, even when there was a move to recruit Gentile converts. Weatherly accepts the verdict of the Gospels of the real responsibility of select Jewish leaders. Yet, he notes, the New Testament records are devoid of any vindictiveness toward the Jewish people.

Two reactions to the Gospel material reflect discontent with the Gospels themselves: Lutheran professor Kysar, mentioned above, for instance, regretted that the Gospel of

John became canonical. Roman Catholic professor, George M. Smiga, who provided a very careful examination of the Gospels agrees with the scholarly consensus that the Gospels attribute Jesus' death to Jewish involvement. Admirably, Smiga patiently amassed the Gospels' evidence on Jewish participation without interjecting critical objections. Yet in his conclusion he distanced himself from the Evangelists' perspective. He wrote:

> We have documented a bias throughout all the gospels which attempts to shift the responsibility for Jesus' death into Jewish hands.....[Yet] such polemics of the past are not part of the Christian gospel we are called to proclaim today....To repudiate the abrogating anti-Judaism of the New Testament does not mean to deny its presence in our tradition. It means that Christian churches choose to disown such anti-Jewish polemic and refuse to accept such beliefs as part of the gospel which we proclaim or as determinative for church life and practice....It is in such times as these that we may, with God's help, find ways to repudiate those parts of our scriptures which demean or insult our Jewish brothers and sisters. It is in such times as these that we may discover that such repudiation will not diminish our scriptures but allow them to emerge more liberated and liberating (George M. Smiga, Pain and Polemic (Anti-Judaism in the Gospels) [Mahwah, NJ: A Stimulus Book, Paulist Press, 1992], pp. 177, 178, 182).

Thus, we have met three responses—recognition (Weatherly), regret that the record exists (Kysar) and repudiation (Smiga). Smiga's opinion should not be left without further comment.

To repudiate the Gospels in the name of the gospel because the combined records render a unanimous indictment of injustice on key Jewish leaders is a ludicrous reaction. Since when does the gospel require us to gloss the records of evil deeds? To dismiss the Gospel accounts because of some embarrassing history risks smearing the credibility of the New Testament canon on every subject it addresses. One cannot insist on loyalty to the veracity and historical accuracy of the Gospel records on other subjects, if the credibility of the records on the life of Christ are suspect. Why should the gospel be believed if the chronicle of that gospel's inception cannot? Beside, the first lesson of the gospel is not refusing to believe that certain men did evil, but that dislike of God's rule by the best of humans shows they need the intervention of divine grace. Both in the gospels and the New Testament epistles the reception of Christ and divine pardon of human guilt are the result of God's sovereign invasion of the human psyche.

NOTES

Chapter 1: Introduction

1. George Whitefield, *Journals* [London: The Banner of Truth Trust, 1960], p. 269.

2. Gerhard Friedrich, *The Theological Dictionary of the New Testament*, translated by Geoffrey W. Bromiley [Grand Rapids: Wm. B. Eerdmans Publishing Co., 1968], 5:840 (B. Reicke). Colin Brown, *Dictionary of New Testament Theology*, H. Esser, 2:438-451 [Grand Rapids: Zondervan Publishing House, 1976].

3. Francis Lyall, *Slaves, Citizens, Sons* (Legal Metaphors in the Epistles) [Grand Rapids: Academic Books, 1984].

4. F. J. Babcock, *The Pauline Epistles and the Epistle to the Hebrews in their Historical Setting* [New York: The Macmillan Co., 1937], p. 184. Also, A. E. Harvey, *Jesus on Trial* [London: SPCK, 1976], pp. 108-110. Worth consulting is the extended note of Raymond E. Brown, *John* (Anchor NT Commentary), vol. 29A (1970), pp. 1135-1144. C. H. Dodd noted that *parakletos*, by the late date of *John*, had 'become a fixed title for the Holy Spirit of the Church' when 'the specific functions of the advocate are not in view.' (*The Interpretation of the Fourth Gospel* [Cambridge, Eng.: University Press, 1953], p.415. Sadly, in Jesus' trials no lawyer was made available to Him, an omission which was in defiance of Jewish law (Josef Blinzler, *The Trial of Jesus*, translated by Isabel and Florence McHugh [Westminster, Maryland: The Newman Press, 1959], p. 135).

5. John Painter, *John, Witness and Theologian* [London: SPCK, 1975], p. 90: 'The evangelist had a trial setting in mind.... The trial portrayed is two-sided. The world had Jesus on trial, but was unable to produce a valid witness. Jesus' witnesses not only cleared Him of all charges: their evidence brought the world under condemnation.'

6. C. H. Dodd, *Interpretation*, op. cit., p. 357.

7. The trial which had most to do with witnesses was before Joseph Caiaphas (see chapter 3); yet, ironically, the Gospel of John

does not record Jesus' appearance before Caiaphas. Rudolf Schnackenburg, *The Gospel According to John*, translated by David Smith and G. A. Kon [New York: The Crossroad Publishing Co., 1982] 3:232, noted that the arguments of the rulers were contained in Christ's appearance before Pilate, so that what the hierarchs said would combine with the pagan hedonists and thereby 'present the one great "case" of Jesus against the unbelieving world.' See pages 78-127 in Allan A. Trites, *The New Testament Concept of Witness* [Cambridge University Press, 1977] and J. M. Boice, *Witness and Revelation in the Gospel of John* [Zondervan, 1970].

8. A. E. Harvey, *Jesus on Trial* op. cit., pp. 14-16.
9. J. Louis Martyn, *History and Theology in the Fourth Gospel*, 2nd ed. revised and enlarged [Nashville: Abingdon, 1979], pp. 66, 156-157. Three distinct stages existed: 1. The sharp examination (including beatings); 2. The excommunication; 3. The execution.
10. A. N. Sherwin-White, *Roman Society and Roman Law in the New Testament* [Grand Rapids: Baker Book House, 1978 (1963)], pp. 27, 28.
11. Blinzler, op. cit., pp. 14, 15, 168. G. Rosadi, *The Trial of Jesus* [New York: Dodd, Mead, and Co., 1905], was among the early writers on the trials who held that Pilate never did pass a sentence on Jesus.
12. Harold W. Hoehner, *Herod Antipas* [Grand Rapids: Zondervan Publishing House, 1980 (1972)], p. 234.
13. Blinzler, op. cit., pp. 168, 239, 243.
14. 'Of a private, rather than of a legal nature,' Blinzler, op. cit., p. 83.
15. Frederick Godet, *The Gospel of John* [Grand Rapids: Zondervan Publishing Co., n.d. (1893)], 2:364.
16. Blinzler, op. cit., p. 91.
17. Joachim Jeremias, *Jerusalem in the Time of Jesus* [Philadelphia: Fortress Press, 1969], pp. 223-267; Frank John Powell, *The Trial of Christ* [London: The Paternoster Press, 1948], p. 62; Alan Hugh McNeile, *The Gospel according to Matthew* [Grand Rapids: Baker Book House, 1982 (1915)], p.

400; David Smith, *The Days of His Flesh* [New York: George H. Doran Co., n.d.], pp. 468-472.

18. Archibald T. Robertson, *Epochs in the Life of Simon Peter* [New York: Charles Scribner's Sons, 1933], p. 135. Also, C. H. Dodd, *The Founder of Christianity* [New York: The MacMillan Company, 1970], p. 157.

19. Blinzler, op. cit., p. 170.

20. Ellis Rivkin, *What Crucified Jesus?* (The Political Execution of a Charismatic) [New York: Abington Press, 1984]. Rivkin viewed Josephus as more reliable than the New Testament documents. For his low view of Scripture, see pp. 66, 67, 91-94, 112-114. *John* is singled out in pp. 91-94. This evaluation of *John* is shared by some neo-Protestants, such as the late S. G. F. Brandon of the University of Manchester, who, in *The Trial of Jesus of Nazareth* [New York: Stein and Day, 1968], pp. 125, 129-132, expressed similar doubts about the value of *John*. Much earlier, in Germany, Hans Lietzmann [1875–1942] considered *John* unhistorical, as well as the entire Jewish trial (see A. N. Sherwin-White's response, op. cit., pp. 32-47).

21. Rivkin, *What Crucified*, op. cit., p. 91.

22. Blinzler, op. cit., p. 40.

23. Rivkin, *What*, op. cit., p. 92.

24. Blinzler, op. cit., pp. 45-47. Quote from p. 46.

25. A. N. Sherwin-White, *Roman Society and Roman Law*, op. cit., p. 47.

26. See the two volume set of C. H. Dodd, *The Interpretation of the Fourth Gospel* [Cambridge University Press, 1953] and *Historical Tradition in the Fourth Gospel* [Cambridge University Press, 1963], especially p. 120. Leon Morris, *Studies in the Fourth Gospel*, [1969], pp. 65-167. Oscar Cullmann, *The Johannine Circle* [Phila.: The Westminster Press, 1976], pp. 13, 20-22, 25, 66, 74, 87, 88.

Raymond E. Brown on the historical question in *John* in his *New Testament Essays* [1965], pp. 143-167, as well as his two volume Anchor Commentary on *John*. Brown says, 'With all its drama and its theology, John's account of the trial [before Pilate] is the most consistent and intelligible we have. Only

John makes it clear why Jesus was brought to Pilate in the first place and why Pilate gave in and had Jesus crucified' (2:861).

Some have questioned, for instance, John's reliability because Pilate went outside the praetorium and returned. On this Blinzler has written: 'As for the outer framework ... it cannot be maintained that the several changes of place in John are historically unthinkable or irreconcilable with the synoptic account' (op. cit., p. 185; see also p. 88 on the reasons for the omission of the Caiaphas court in John).

27. Blinzler, op. cit., pp. 42, 43. In *The Gospel of John* the frequent expression 'the Jews' is a narrowing of opposition as coming from high-ranking Jewish officials, which epitomized, quite tragically, the world-spirit hostile to God (cf. John 15:25 with v.18). C. H. Dodd has written: 'The statement, which is often made, that the Johannine account is influenced by the motive of incriminating the Jews cannot be substantiated, when it is compared with other gospels.' (*Historical Tradition in the Fourth Gospel* [Cambridge: Cambridge University Press, 1963], p. 107).

S. G. F. Brandon held that Mark 'pioneered' (op. cit., pp. 107, 112) the view of Jewish-leadership involvement in Christ's death and that Matthew made Jews 'exclusively guilty' of it (p. 115).

Gregory Baum, *Is the New Testament Anti-Semitic?* [Glen Rock: Paulist Press, 1965], p. 137: 'John's alleged anti-semitism is only apparent, that he manifests neither bias nor resentment against the people of Israel, and to find in the gospel the justification of a contemptuous attitude toward the Jewish people is to misunderstand completely the intention of the evangelist.' Again, Baum wrote, 'There is an extraordinary harshness in John, but this severity is not in the least directed against the synagogue; it represents rather the devastating judgment of God on all that is wickedness, falsehood and hatred' (ibid., p. 138).

Raymond E. Brown, referred to above, insisted to a *Newsweek* reporter that John's polemics were theological thrusts against Judaism, not ethnic slurs. 'Bad as it is, anti-

Judaism is not the same thing as anti-Semitism' (*Newsweek*, April 23, 1973, p. 72; see his *Commentary on John*, 2:792-800 on this question).

Rudolf Schnackenburg wrote on John's alleged anti-semitism: 'In John's Gospel there is, with all the polemic against the leaders of Judaism, no condemnation of the entire Jewish nation, rather, a continuing appeal to Jewish people to believe in Jesus the Messiah and Son of God. But John too draws a clear line of distinction: that Judaism which rejects its true king of salvation is, for him, lost to the salvific rule of God.'

Although we cannot go so far as Canon H. P. Liddon in ignoring the Jewish character of the opposition in John, nevertheless, we agree with the bottom-line of what he says concerning the centrality of Christ. Liddon was representative of the move by many nineteenth century commentators to de-Jewize the expression 'the Jews'. He said the expression 'ignores the differences of character, class, and sect among them, and notices them only so far as they are in conflict with the central truth manifested in Jesus' (*The Divinity of our Lord and Saviour Jesus Christ* [London: Rivingtons, 1889 (1867)], p. 226). We must continue to recognize the historicity of the expression 'the Jews', yet realize that they were just ordinary men and sinners like the rest of us.

28. Blinzler, op. cit., p. 31. Moreover, even outside the New Testament, material in Judaism shows that the climate against Jesus' movement was more savage than some would like to admit. On this C. K. Barrett cites the bitter maledictions against the Nazarene movement at the time of *The Gospel of John* (*The Gospel of John and Judaism* [Phila.: Fortress Press, 1975], pp. 47-48, for examples). See pp. 169-171 in Giovanni Rosadi, *The Trial of Jesus* [New York: Dodd, Mead, and Co., 1905] for more extra-biblical material on Christ's trials.

29. S. G. F. Brandon, *The Trial of Jesus of Nazareth* [New York: Stein and Day, 1968], pp. 107, 112.

30. Harold Cooke Phillips, *In the Light of the Cross* [New York: Abingdon Press, 1947], p. 11.

Chapter 2: Christ Before Annas

1. F. F. Bruce, *The Gospel of John* [Grand Rapids: Wm. B. Eerdmans Publishing Co., 1983], p. 343.
2. W. R. Wilson, *The Execution of Jesus* [New York: Charles Scribner's Sons, 1970], p. 177.
3. Klaas Schilder, *The Trial of Christ* [Grand Rapids: Wm. B. Eerdmans Publishing Co., 1939], p. 20.
4. David Smith, *The Days of His Flesh* [New York: George H. Doran Company, n.d.], p. 463. Blinzler, op. cit., pp. 183, 189. The historical circumstances of the Roman appointment of the high priest strongly favors the likelihood of the-off-the-record meeting. John H. Bernard, *John* (International Critical Commentary) [Edinburgh: T & T Clark, 1928], 2:606-607, who admits prior knowledge, but not necessarily a previous secret meeting. Raymond E. Brown, however, says that the ten year reign of Caiaphas meant 'the two men must have been able to work together when it served their purpose' (*John* Commentary, op. cit., 2:798). J. Duncan M. Derrett, *Law in the New Testament* [London: Darton, Longman & Todd, 1970], p. 436: 'Pilate, about whom a great deal is known, would not believe in doing something for nothing. That he took bribes from Caiaphas seems certain. The way to handle Jews was to keep on top of them. To feel the pulse of public life ... Pilate must have had informers, spies and advisers, and can have had more than an inkling of what was going on.'
5. Frank Morison, *Who Moved the Stone?* [Grand Rapids: Zondervan Publishing, 1970 (1930)], p. 40, see also, pp. 43-59.
6. Frank J. Powell, *The Trial of Christ* [London: The Paternoster Press, 1948], p. 85.
7. Schilder, op. cit., p. 19, 41.
8. A. E. Harvey, *Jesus on Trial* [London: SPCK, 1976], p. 62.
9. Ernst Bammel, *The Trial of Jesus*, edited by E. Bammel [London: SCM Press Ltd., 1970], p. 29.
10. Schilder, op. cit., p. 20.
11. Joseph Blinzler, *The Trial of Jesus*, 2nd rev. ed., translated by Florence and Isabel McHugh [Westminster, Maryland: The

Newman Press, 1959], p. 83. Raymond E. Brown, *The Anchor Bible, The Gospel of John* [Garden City, NY: Doubleday and Company, 1970] 29A: 823.

12. C. Kopp, *The Holy Places of the Gospels* [Freiburg: Herder, 1963], pp. 352-361.

13. R. M. Mockowski, *Jerusalem: City of Jesus* [Grand Rapids: Wm. B. Eerdmans Publishing Co., 1978], p. 165. N. Avigad, *Archaeological Discoveries in the Jewish Quarter of Jerusalem* [Jerusalem: Israel's Exploration Society, 1976].

14. Blinzler, op. cit., p. 84. The New International Version of 18:24 ('still bound') may suggest that Christ was bound during the interview. I think, however, the intent of the narrator was to point out that Jesus' captors did not trust His security between point A and point B.

15. Frederich Godet, *The Gospel of John* [Grand Rapids: Zondervan Publishing House, n.d. (1893, 3rd ed.) 1:301–302. See especially Joachim Jeremias, *Jerusalem in the Time of Jesus* [Phila.: Fortress Press, 1969], pp.147-270.

16. Blinzler, op. cit., p. 83.

17. ibid., p. 82.

18. ibid., p. 94.

19. Richard Lenski, *The Interpretation of Matthew* [Minneapolis, MN: Augsburg Publishing House, 1943], p. 813. Frank John Powell, *The Trial of Christ* [London: The Paternoster Press, 1948], p. 56: 'The House of Annas derived much of its wealth from the business side of the Temple activities. The cleansing of the Temple was a direct interference by Jesus with the authority of Annas and his class.' See William Lane, *Commentary on Mark* (New International Critical Commentary) [Grand Rapids: Wm. B. Eerdmans Publishing Co., 1974], p. 403 on the lucrative operations of Annas and Caiaphas in the 'sacrificial animal mart'.

20. Blinzler, op. cit., p. 52.

21. Flavius Josephus, *Complete Works*, translated by William Whiston [Grand Rapids: Kregel Publications, 1978], *Antiquities of the Jews*, xiv, 9.4, page 298.

22. Blinzler, op. cit., p. 86.

23. Thomas Brooks, *Heaven on Earth* [London: The Banner of Truth Trust, 1961 (1654)], p. 268.

Chapter 3: Christ Before Caiaphas

1. Alan H. McNeile, *The Gospel of Matthew* [Grand Rapids: Baker Book House, 1982 (1915)], p. 398. Alfred Edersheim, *The Life and Times of Jesus the Messiah* [New York: Anson D. F. Randolph and Company, 1886], 2:554, 555.

2. A. M. Fairbairn, *Studies in the Life of Christ* [London: Hodder and Stoughton, 1882], p. 288.

3. James Stalker, *The Trial and Death of Jesus Christ* [New York: A. C. Armstrong and Son, 1906], p. 18. Giovanni Rosadi, *The Trial of Christ*, op. cit., p. 123: 'The real sacerdotal authority lay in the hands of [Annas].' F. W. Farrar, *The Life of Christ* [New York: A. L. Burt Company, 1874], says, Caiaphas was 'endowed with less force of character and will' than Annas (p. 461).

4. Joachim Jeremias, *Jerusalem in the Time of Jesus* [Philadelphia: Fortress Press, 1955, (1969)], p. 157.

5. William M. Clow, *The Day of the Cross* [London: Hodder and Stoughton, 1910], p. 15.

6. Blinzler, op. cit., p. 91.

7. *Mishnah*, 'Sanhedrin', 7:5.

8. Jeremias, op. cit., p. 157.

9. Edersheim, op. cit., 2:561. Matthew 26:65 refers to the rending of the outer garment (toga) and Mark 14:63 to the rending of the inner garment (tunic). 'Not everybody wore inner garments or shirts (chitones) or if they did, wore more than one' (Mk. 6:9; Matt. 10:10), says Alfred Plummer, *The Gospel of Matthew* [Grand Rapids: Baker Book House, 1982 (1915)], p. 380.

10. McNeile, op. cit., pp. 397, 398.

11. Blinzler, op. cit., p. 110. Between AD 6 and 37 the vestments of the high priest were held in safe keeping in the Fortress of Antonia and only given out for the liturgical functions of the feast days. Although Christ was tried on the eve of the Passover, it is unlikely that Caiaphas was occupied about wearing the right clothes and because of the inconvenience of distance and

Roman rules, it is unlikely that Caiaphas wore his expensive and elaborate high priestly robe during the abbreviated session of the Sanhedrin in his quarters. But it is most probable that he put them on for the ratification session the next morning in the Hall of Hewn Stone.

12. McNeile, op. cit., p. 402. David Smith, *The Days of His Flesh* (op. cit., p. 471) was one who took it that Caiaphas was play acting. 'It was no involuntary manifestation of horror but a histrionic conventionality. His emotion was a mere pretence.'

13. William Cowper, *Works* [New York: W. I. Pooley, 1848], 'The Task', Bk. 6, p. 601a.

14. Ellis Rivkin, *What Crucified Jesus?* op. cit., pp. 48, 53, 87, 117, 120, 124.

15. William O. Douglas, *The Court Years (1931–1975)* [New York: Vintage Books, 1981], pp. 7-9. For additional material on the human element of the justices of the Supreme Court in the years between 1969-1975, see Bob Woodward and Scott Armstrong, *The Brethren* [New York: Simon and Schuster, 1979].

16. Blinzler, op. cit., p. 106. C. H. Dodd, however, thought that Jesus' identification with God was 'what the charge of "blasphemy" really stands for, rather than any definable statutory offence' (*More New Testament Studies* [Grand Rapids: Wm. W. Eerdmans Publishing Co., 1968], p. 99). But this cannot have been the Jewish view then, for otherwise they would have tried to argue it before Pilate, who could understand a visitation from God better than Jews. Of course, they did try that approach (John 19:7) as one of the last pressure tactics to have Pilate sentence Jesus to die. As Rudolf Bultmann has argued, at this point, 'they adduce a reason for their demand that must be plausible to him' (*The Gospel of John*, A Commentary, translated by G. R. Beasley-Murray, R. W. N. Hoare and J. K. Riches [Philadelphia: Westminster Press, 1971], p. 660). If it was understandable in Pilate's second trial, it would have been understandable at the start of the first. Therefore, C. H. Dodd's position lacks force.

17. McNeile, op. cit., p. 403.

18. Ibid., p. 399.
19. Frank J. Powell, *The Trial of Christ* [London: The Paternoster Press, 1948], p. 65, (citing the *Mishnah* 6:1, 2, 3, 4 of tractate 'Sanhedrin', with Deut. 17:7).
20. Ibid., p. 70.
21. Alexander T. Innes, *The Trial of Christ* [Edinburgh: T & T Clark, 1899], p. 56.
22. McNeile, op. cit., p. 400.
23. Wm. M. Clow, *The Day of the Cross*, op. cit., p. 18. Alexander McLaren, *Expositions of Holy Scripture* (11 volume edition, 1952, Eerdmans Publishing Co.) vol. 7, sec. 2: 110: says of Caiaphas – 'A crafty schemer, and blind as a mole to the beauty of Christ's character and the greatness of His words, utterly unspiritual, undisguisedly selfish, rude as a boar, cruel as a cutthroat.'
24. Blinzler, op. cit., p. 227.
25. Henry Harbaugh, *The Golden Censor* [Philadelphia: The Publication and Sunday School Society Board of the Reformed Church in the U.S., 1860], pp. 257, 258.
26. Klaas Schilder, *The Trial of Christ*, op. cit., p. 178.

Chapter 4: Christ Before Pilate

1. Mark contains many of Jesus' rebukes to silence (1:25, 34; 3:12) and many of His commands to silence (1:43-45; 5:43; 7:36; 8:26). His commands to silence reflected positively on his position as God's Son. Ralph Martin has written: 'The commands to silence and the rebukes administered to demons are proof of his divine authority and a sign of his destiny to remain on earth as an unrecognised, unclaimed Redeemer-figure' (*Mark: Evangelist and Theologian* [Grand Rapids: Zondervan Publishing House, 1973], p. 101. See also pp. 148, 149, where Martin argues that Jesus' commands to silence, *when violated*, show the profound reality of His stature as deity.)
2. Harold W. Hoehner, *Herod Antipas*, op. cit., pp. 199, 200; see his appendix: 'The Withdrawals of Jesus', pp. 317-330.
3. Three jurisdiction/place matters arise during the trials:
   A. The locations for the hearing before Annas and for the grand

jury type examination before the Sanhedrin in executive session attract interest. Many favour the palace of Caiaphas, for it allowed privacy and had plenty of space, both for Christ's examination by Annas and by Caiaphas.

John 18:15 mentions the high priest's courtyard. It was an open space where a fire could be used to warm the palace personnel on a chilly night.

This physical feature makes a point about its size. Several places are suggested as the probable building and location – See Raymond E. Brown, *John* vol. 29A. op. cit., p. 823. A palace with a courtyard would allow Jesus to look upon Peter as He passed from one session to another, say from an atrium to an auditorium, in the same building, for it seems that Jesus was examined on the second floor according to Mark 14:66 – 'Peter was below in the courtyard.'

B. Where Pilate tried Jesus has attracted most controversy. Two major locations vie for 'most likely place'. One was the Fortress of Antonia, which was next to the Temple of Herod and the Hall of Hewn Stone, where the Sanhedrin held court. The Fortress housed the military and had a small courtyard and well-outfitted living quarters. The other building was the Palace of Herod, which was on the other side of Old Jerusalem. The evidence for one over the other has been a matter of scholarly debate. For a review of the evidence and argumentation see J. H. Bernard, *John*, International Critical Commentary (1928), 2:605f; Alexander Innes, *The Trial of Christ* (1899), pp. 72, 73; J. Blinzler, *The Trial of Christ* (1959), pp. 173-176; Raymond E. Brown, *John*, Anchor NT Commentary (1970), vol. 29A:845-846; F. F. Bruce, *The Gospel of John* (1983), pp. 348, 349; R. Schnackenburg, *The Gospel of John* (1982), 3:243f.

C. As for the location of Christ's appearance before Herod Antipas there is little doubt that it was the Hasmonean palace. See Harold W. Hoehner, *Herod Antipas*, (1980), p. 239; Joseph A. Fitzmyer, *The Gospel According to Luke*, (1985), vol. 28a:1481.

4. Karl Barth, *Church Dogmatics* II.1 [Edinburgh: T & T Clark, 1957], p. 453.
5. Rudolf Bultmann, *The Gospel of John*, translated by G. R. Beasley-Murray, R. W. N. Hoare, J. K. Riches [Philadelphia: The Westminster Press, 1971], p. 652.
6. Blinzler, op. cit., pp. 181, 183.
7. David Smith, *The Days of His Flesh*, op. cit., p. 478.
8. Blinzler, op. cit., pp. 178, 179.
9. Emil Schurer, *The History of the Jewish People in the Age of Jesus Christ*, op. cit., vol. 1: 386.
10. ibid., 1: 359, 372.
11. ibid., 1: 358.
12. ibid., 1: 372.
13. ibid., 1: 372-375.
14. James I. Packer, M. C. Tenney, William White, Jr., *The Bible Almanac* [Nashville: Thomas Nelson Publishers, 1980], p. 185. For an excellent, brief summary, see J. Jeremias, *Jerusalem in the Time of Jesus*, op. cit., pp. 124-126.
15. Josephus, *Antiquities* 18:3, 1; *War against the Jews*, 2:9, 4.
16. E Schurer, *History of Jewish People*, op. cit., 1: 359, 367.
17. This detail is not found in the other Gospels, but it unlocks the irrationality of sin against God's Son. It reflects a facet of the inner dynamics of hatred for Christ which is important to stress. See Leon Morris's discussion of it in his *Studies in the Fourth Gospel* [Grand Rapids: Wm. B. Eerdmans Publishing Co., 1969], pp. 191-195.
18. A. N. Sherwin-White, *Roman Society and Roman Law in the New Testament,* op. cit., pp. 35, 36, 37.
19. Blinzler, op. cit., pp. 188, 189.
20. H. W. Hoehner, '... The Year of Christ's Crucifixion', *Bibliotheca Sacra*, 131 (1974), pp. 32-348.
21. E. Schurer, op. cit., 1: 384.
22. John Calvin's comments on Christ's sinlessness are still important:

> We make Christ free of all stain not just because he was begotten of his mother without copulation with man, but because he was sanctified by the Spirit.... Whenever

Scripture calls our attention to the purity of Christ, it is to be understood of his true human nature, for it would have been superfluous to say God is pure (*Institutes of the Christian Religion*, Ford Lewis Battles, ed. [Phila.: The Westminster Press, 1960], Bk II; 13:4, vol. 1: 481).

Wolfhart Pannenberg, in his *Jesus, God and Man*, revised ed. [Phila.: The Westminster Press, 1977], p. 355:

If sin is essentially life in contradiction to God, in self-centred closing off our ego against God, then Jesus' unity with God in his personal community with the Father and in his identity with the person of the Son of God means immediately his separation from all sin.

See also pp. 357, 358, 361, 362. For another modern theologian affirming Christ's sinlessness, see Karl Barth, *Church Dogmatics*, I.2 (1939), pp. 40, 152-158; II.1 (1957), p. 397. For older works see Carl Ullmann, *The Sinlessness of Jesus* [Edinburgh: T & T Clark, 1901]; Henry P. Liddon, *Passiontide Sermons* [New York: Longmans, Green and Co., 1898], pp. 1-17.

23. William Cowper, *Works*, Grimshawe edition, op. cit., p. 578 ('The Task').

Chapter 5: Christ Before Herod Antipas

1. Emil Schurer, *The History of the Jewish People in the Age of Jesus Christ*, New English version, revised and edited by G. Vermes and F. Millar [Edinburgh: T & T Clark, Ltd, 1973], I:357.

2. ibid., II:357-398.

3. J. I. Packer, Merrill C. Tenney, William White, Jr., *The Bible Almanac* [Nashville: Thomas Nelson Publishers, 1980], p. 185.

4. Joseph Addison Alexander, *Commentary on Mark* [Grand Rapids: Baker Book House, 1980 (1858)], p. 151.

5. ibid.

6. A. van den Born, *Encyclopedic Dictionary of the Bible*, 2nd revised ed., by Louis F. Hartman [New York: McGraw-Hill Book Company, Inc. 1963], p. 1048

7. Josephus, *Antiquities of the Jews*, op. cit., 15:2.

8. Samuel Sandmel, *Herod, Profile of a Tyrant* [Philadelphia: J. B. Lippincott Co., 1967], pp. 87, 117.

9. Harold W. Hoehner, *Herod Antipas, a Contemporary of Jesus Christ* [Grand Rapids: Zondervan Publishing House, 1980 (1972)], p. 11.

10. The orator, poet and historian was Asinius Pollio, friendly towards Jews and a Jew himself.

11. E. Schurer, op. cit., I: 343.

12. ibid.

13. William M. Ramsay, *St. Paul the Traveller and the Roman Citizen* [London: Hodder and Stoughton, 1896], p. 388.

14. H. W. Hoehner, op. cit., p. 249.

15. H. W. Hoehner, op. cit., p. 245.

16. ibid., pp. 84-109.

17. Alexander Whyte, *Bible Characters,* 4th Series [Grand Rapids: Zondervan Publishing House, 1967], p. 81.

18. J. Blinzler, op. cit., p. 198.

19. ibid. *lese majestas* was the crime of treason, for which Pilate began his trial of Jesus. 'But Herod Antipas was too prudent to meddle in a charge of *majestas*. He turned the matter into a pleasant pantomime by arraying Jesus in "gorgeous apparel" ' (p. 15, Herbert B. Workman, *Persecution in the Early Church* [Nashville: Abington Press, 1960 (1906)]).

20. J. Blinzler, op. cit., p. 199, note 11; H. W. Hoehner, op. cit., p. 243; Kittel, *The Theological Dictionary of the New Testament*, vols. 4:217, 27; 7:687-691.

21. Josephus, *Antiquities*, op. cit., 19:344.

22. H. W. Hoehner, op. cit., p. 243.

23. J. Blinzler, op. cit., p. 199.

24. ibid.

25. Ernst Bammel, *The Trial of Jesus*, edited by J. E. Allen [London: SCM, 1970], p. 89.

26. Rudolf Schnackenburg, *The Gospel According to John* op. cit., III: 274.

27. Malcolm Muggeridge, *The End of Christendom* [Grand Rapids: Wm. B. Eerdmans Publishing Co., 1980], p. 2.

Chapter 6: Christ Before Pilate

1. I. Howard Marshall, *Last Supper and Lord's Supper* [Grand Rapids: Wm. B. Eerdmans Publishing Co., 1980], p. 75. F. Godet, *John*, op. cit., 2: 379, 380. Especially thorough and recent is Leon Morris's additional note, 'The Lord's Supper and the Passover', *John*, op. cit., pp. 774-786. He says, 'The idea that the Lord's Supper was not the Passover, but a meal of some sort ... cannot be ruled out absolutely' (p. 781). What suggests more flexibility on the observation patterns of that era, according to Strack-Billerbeck, is that Pharisees and Sadducees used slightly different calendars. See also E. Stauffer, *Jesus and His Story* [London, 1960].

2. J. H. Bernard, *John* (ICC), op. cit., 1: cii (see the section on Chronology, pp. cii-cviii). Some forty-seven years later Oscar Cullmann voiced the same conviction in his *The Johannine Circle* [Phila.: The Westminster Press, 1976 (1975)], p. 66: 'At many points the passion narrative ... seems to have greater historical value than that of the synoptics.'

3. See Theodor Zahn [1838–1933], *Introduction to the New Testament* [Grand Rapids: Kregel Publications, 1953 (1909)], 3: 273-283, 296-298. Harold W. Hoehner, *Chronological Aspects of the Life of Christ* [Grand Rapids: Zondervan Publishing House, 1977], pp. 76-90. Rudolf Schnackenburg, *The Gospel According to John*, op. cit., 3: 33-47 (Excursus 15 – 'The Johannine Last Supper and its Problems'). I. Howard Marshall, *Last Supper, Lord's Supper*, op. cit., pp. 68-75, 133-139.

4. 'Hour' in *John*: esp. 2:4; 7:6, 8, 30; 8:20; also 12:23, 27; 17:1; 19:25–27. 'Hour' still to come 2:4; 4:21, 23; 5:25, 28; 6:30; 8:20; 16:2, 25, 32 which sees Jesus looking ahead to His final ordeal/triumph and in His victory continuing in His church. On the use of 'hour' see Raymond E. Brown, *John*, op. cit., vol. 29 (1966): 517-518.

   Oscar Cullmann, *Johannine Circle*, op. cit., p. 21, 22 commented on this subject: 'Everything that happens in the Gospel narratives takes place according to a foreordained divine 'timetable', as one might almost call it. During this brief period of activity every moment is of supreme significance for the salvation of the world. His brothers (7:8) are free to ... go up to Jerusalem at any time. Jesus, on the other hand, must wait for the particular moment for each of his works.... Thus according to John 9:2ff, the reason why the blind man was to be *born* blind must be sought not in a sin committed by himself or his parents, but in the divine necessity for Jesus to meet him at this moment and in this particular place to heal him.'

J. Blinzler, op. cit., pp. 288, 289: 'When the Passion is traced back to the will of God and of Jesus, or to the activities of Satan and his diabolic forces, it is in no wise intended thereby to dispute or even to minimize the guilt of those historically responsible.' See Benjamin B. Warfield, *The Works of Benjamin B. Warfield* [Grand Rapids: Baker Book House, 1981 (1929)], vol. 2: 35-39 for predestination in *John*. Rudolf Schnackenburg, *John*, 2: 259-274 (Excursus # 11). A fuller treatment is found in D. A. Carson's 1975 Cambridge University doctoral dissertation, *Divine Sovereignty and Human Responsibility* (Biblical perspectives in tension) [Atlanta: John Knox Press, 1981].

5. F. Godet, *John*, 2:377; F. J. Powell, *The Trial of Christ*, op. cit., pp. 117, 118; J. H. Bernard, *John*, op. cit., 2:613.

6. J. Blinzler, op. cit., p. 208.

7. C. H. Dodd, *The Founder of Christianity* [London: The Macmillan Co., 1970], p. 161.

8. E. Schurer, *The History of the Jewish People*, op. cit., 1: 362.

9. Sherwin-White, *Roman Law*, op. cit., pp. 27, 28. Of particular interest is the article of Roy A. Stewart, 'Judicial Procedure in New Testament Times,' *The Evangelical Quarterly*, vol. 47, No. 2, April-June, 1975, pp. 94-109. In it is a summary of the punishment system used in first-century synagogues, both verbal and physical. Romans and Jews both used rods. The Roman rods are known to those familiar with the tied bundle of rods and protruding medial axe. 'Pilate and Jerusalem may have lacked this' instrument of punishment (ibid., p. 98). Jesus felt the Roman *flagellum*. 'Synagogue scourgings were less fiendishly brutal than their Roman equivalents, and their ideal

intention was reformatory rather than merely punitive – but they can scarcely be described as humane, and the potential of abuse was ever present' (ibid., p. 99). Mr. Stewart also pointed out, 'Though the rod was not unknown in Rabbinic procedure, it was customary to use the three-tongued leather strap, and to administer the celebrated "forty stripes save one"' (ibid).

10. D. Smith, *In the Days*, op. cit., p. 487.

11. J. Jeremias, *Jerusalem*, op. cit., pp. 58-84; the Excursus, 'The Number of Pilgrims at the Passover', pp. 77-84.

12. ibid., pp. 60-62.

13. Rollo May, *Love and Will* [New York: Dell Publishing, 1974 (1969)], p. 160.

14. *am ha ares* means 'people of the land'. For instances, see Matthew 9:10, 11; 11:19; Mark 2:16 (earliest reference); Luke 5:30, 34; 15:2; 19:7; John 7:49. Rudolf Meyer, *Theological Dictionary of the New Testament*, op. cit., 5 (1967): 589, 590; Jeremias, *Jerusalem*, op. cit., pp. 105, 249, 259, 266f; Martin Hengel, *The Charismatic Leader and His Followers* [New York: Crossroad, 1981], p. 68.

15. John Chrysostom, *Nicene and Post Nicene Fathers* [Grand Rapids: Wm. B. Eerdmans Publishing Co., 1983 (1888)], 14:373. Blinzler held that 'Behold the Man' by Pilate was his attempt to demonstrate Jesus' harmlessness (op. cit., p. 229). Pilate knew that Jesus was considered harmful. He was presented harmed, not harmless.

16. Leon Morris, *John*, op. cit., p. 793. Robert B. Whyte, *The Sins that Crucified Jesus* [New York: Fleming H. Revell Co., 1937], p. 71, described it as being 'admiration mingled with pity'.

17. Morris, op. cit., p. 792.

18. John Marsh, *The Gospel of St. John* [Baltimore, MD: Penguin Books, 1968], p. 606.

19. W. E. Sangster, *They Met at Calvary* [New York: Abingdon, 1956], p. 43.

20. Walter Bauer, William F. Arndt, Felix Gingrich, Frederick W. Danker, *A Greek-English Lexicon of the New Testament* 2nd ed. [Chicago: The University of Chicago, 1979], p. 449.

21. B. B. Warfield, *Select Shorter Works*, op. cit., 2:690.

22. F. Godet, *John*, op. cit., 2:377; George Reith, *The Gospel of John* [Edinburgh: T & T Clark Ltd., n.d.] 2:143; J. Stalker, *Trial*, op. cit., p. 109; Packer, Tenney, White, Jr., *Bible Almanac*, op. cit., p. 185.
23. William Cowper, *Works*, op. cit., p. 542 ('Hope').
24. Mary Ann Sidebotham, source unknown.
25. Hugh Martin, ed., *A Treasury of Christian Verse* [Philadelphia: Fortress Press, 1959], p. 30.

Appendix One

1. Colin Cross, *Who was Jesus?* [New York: Atheneum, 1970], pp. 98, 99.
2. Ernst Bammel, ed., *The Trial of Jesus* [London: SCM, 1970], p. 94.
3. Josef Blinzler, *The Trial of Jesus*, op. cit., pp. 17-20.
4. ibid., p. 15.
5. ibid., pp. 16, 17.
6. *Time*, 11/10/67, p. 76; Haim Cohen, *The Trial and Death of Jesus* [New York: Harper and Row, 1971], pp. 419; see Edwin Yamauchi's review of Cohen's work, *Christianity Today*, 9/10/71.
7. J. Duncan M. Derrett, *Law in the New Testament* [London: Darton, Longman, and Todd, Ltd., 1970], p. 417.
8. John Warwick Montgomery, 'Jesus Takes the Stand: An Argument to Support the Gospel Accounts,' *Christianity Today*, April 9, 1982.
9. Blinzler, op. cit., p. 139.
10. Derrett, op. cit., p. 418, in which he runs through several cases of Pharisaic support.
11. Rodney A. Whitacre, *Johannine Polemics* [Chico, CA: Scholars Press, 1982 (1980)], p. 118.
12. Rudolf Schnackenburg, *Commentary on the Gospel of John*, op. cit., 3:407.
13. Francis Lyall, *Slaves, Citizens, and Sons,* op. cit., pp. 191-200.
14. ibid., p. 204.
15. ibid., p. 204. Edwin Yamauchi, 'Historical Notes on the Trial and Crucifixion of Jesus Christ,' *Christianity Today*, April 9, 1971.

16. Lyall, op. cit., p. 205.

17. Blinzler in E. Bammel, ed., *Trial*, op. cit., p. 152.

18. Josephus, *Antiquities*, 13:294f.

19. Derrett, op. cit., p. 393. Contrast his view of Powell with James Moffatt's view of Innes' volume, *Dictionary of Christ and the Gospels*, 2:759a.

20. Derrett, op. cit., p. xxiv.

21. W. R. Wilson, *The Execution of Jesus*, op. cit., p. 10.

22. Derrett, op. cit., p. 436.

23. Blinzler, op. cit., pp. 143, 149-157.

24. C. H. Dodd, *Interpretation of the Fourth Gospel*, op. cit., p. 37.

25. Blinzler, op. cit., p. 7.

26. ibid., p. 157.

27. Joachim Jeremias, *Jerusalem in the Time of Jesus*, op. cit., pp. 223, 224; H. F. Weiss, *TDNT*, op. cit. 9:37; William Barclay, *The Gospel of John* [Philadelphia: The Westminster Press, 1956], 2:120, 121.

28. Blinzler, op. cit., p. 145, where he questioned whether there was a separate morning sitting of the court.

29. ibid., p. 138.

30. R. W. Husband tabulated twenty-seven violations of Mishnaic Law (which he did not accept, however, as having occurred). See Blinzler, op. cit., p. 137; R. E. Brown, *John*, Anchor, op. cit., 2:796.

31. ibid., 2:799.

32. F. J. Powell, *The Trial of Christ* op. cit., 70.

33. ibid., p. 65.

34. Blinzler, op. cit., p. 239.

35. Sherwin-White, *Roman Law*, op. cit., p. 36; D. R. Catchpole in E. Bammel, ed., *The Trial of Jesus*, op. cit., p. 63. See Leon Morris, *The Gospel of John*, op. cit., Excursus, 'Roman and Jewish Law,' pp. 786-788.

36. Alan Hugh McNeile, *The Gospel according to Matthew*, op. cit., p. 398.

37. *TalJer, Sanhedrin*, I, 18a, 34; 7:24b, 41, cited in R. E. Brown, op. cit., 2:850; also noted by W. R. Wilson, op. cit., p. 14.

38. Blinzler, op. cit., p. 165.
39. ibid., p. 124.
40. James Moffatt, 'The Trial of Jesus,' *The Dictionary of Christ and the Gospels*, edited by James Hastings [Edinburgh: T & T Clark, 1909], 2:749.
41. Blinzler, op. cit., p. 169.
42. R. E. Brown, op. cit., 2:849, 850, and the major commentaries on the *Acts* 7 passage.

Appendix Two

1. A. H. McNeile, *Gospel according to Matthew*, op. cit., p. 300.
2. J. H. Bernard, *John,* ICC, op. cit., 1:88.
3. E. F. Scott, *The Crisis in the Life of Jesus* [New York: Charles Scribner's Sons, 1952], p. 18.
4. Leon Morris, *John,* op. cit., p. 157.
5. Raymond E. Brown, *John*, Anchor Commentary, op. cit., 1:118.
6. Donald Guthrie, *New Testament Introduction* [Downers Grove, IL: Intervarsity Press, 1970], p.293; Alfred Plummer, *Matthew*, op. cit., p.287.
7. R. V. G. Tasker, *The Gospel According to Matthew*, Tyndale New Testament Commentary [Grand Rapids: Wm. B. Eerdmans Publishing Co., 1960], p. 61.
8. C. H. Dodd, *Historical Tradition in the Fourth Gospel,* op. cit., p. 162.
9. J. Julius Scott, Jr., *Dictionary of New Testament Theology,* ed. C. Brown [Grand Rapids: Zondervan Publishing House, 1978], 3:440.

Appendix Three

1. *The Anchor Bible Dictionary* (Vol. 1 [A-C], [New York: Doubleday, 1992], pp.257-258, 803-806)
2. J. Blinzler, *The Trial of Jesus* [Cork: The Mercier Press, Ltd., 1959], pp. 49, 291
3. Adolf Schlatter [1852–1938], *The History of the Christ*, translated by Andreas J. Kostenberger, 1997 [Grand Rapids: Baker Books, 1923, 1997], p. 367.

SELECTED BIBLIOGRAPHY

The following works – for the most part – honor the historical reliability or accuracy of the Four Gospels.

Besser, Wilhelm F., *The Passion Story* (Minneapolis, 1847, 1953)

Blinzler, Josef, *The Trial of Jesus* (Westminster, MD, 1959)

Brown, Raymond, *The Death of the Messiah* (Garden City, NY, 2 vols., 1994)

Catchpole, David, *The Trial of Jesus* (Leiden, 1971)

Chandler, David C., *The Trial of Jesus from a Lawyer's Standpoint* (NY, 1925, 2 vols.), reprinted by The Harrison Co., Norcross, GA, USA, 1976.

Hoehner, Harold W., *Herod Antipas* (Grand Rapids, 1972)

Innes, A. Taylor, *The Trial of Jesus Christ* (Edinburgh, 1899)

Imbert, Jean, *Le Proces de Jesus* (Paris, 1980)

Krummacher, Frederick W., *The Suffering Savior* (New York, 1855)

Linton, O., *Sanhedrin Verdict* (New York, 1943)

Morison, Frank, *Who Moved the Stone* (London, 1930)

Powell, Frank J., *The Trial of Christ* (London, 1948)

Rosadi, Giovanni, *The Trial of Jesus* (New York, 1905)

Schilder, Klaas, *Christ on Trial* (Grand Rapids, 1939)

Stalker, James, *The Trial and Death of Jesus Christ* (New York, 1906)

Dr. John Gilmore, a second-generation Welsh preacher, has resided in Cincinnati, Ohio, US since 1982. He speaks at Conferences and church Seminars in the areas of his five books (eschatology, the passion narratives of the Gospels, and spiritual concerns of senior citizens). In July 2000, at Spurgeon's School of Theology, London, he lectured on heaven, the subject of his first book, which after four printings in the US has been reprinted in the UK. His five books are *Probing Heaven* (Key Questions on the Hereafter), UK reprint; also available in Korean; *Too Young To Be Old* (Secrets from Bible Seniors on How to Live Long and Well); *Ambushed At Sunset* (Coping with Mature Adult Temptations); *Lotto: Fun or Folly?*; *The Trials of Christ* (Moral Failings in Four Judges).